pro ge ny \ prä-jə-nē \
    1. offspring, descendants, children, successors

Snails Are Nocturnal

short stories & poems

Jon McMaster

Library of Congress Control Number: 2009914255
ISBN: Hardcover   978-1-4500-2223-1
                 Softcover   978-1-4500-2222-4

Print information available on the last page.

This collection was edited by Marina Smith.

Cover design by Melissa Foliente.
Cover photo by Kimberly Wassenberg.
Author photo by Valerie MacRae.

To order additional copies of this book, contact:
Xlibris
1-888-795-4274
www.Xlibris.com
Orders@Xlibris.com
40468

Acknowledgements

This collection would be yet unpublished without the love and persistence of two brilliant friends: Marina Smith and Randy Foliente.

Thank you, Marina—as an Editor, your wordsmithing is precise. I'm grateful for your unwillingness to concede to my impatience and for sending me back to the keyboard when necessary. You hear what is missing. Thank you for holding me accountable to my best work and for valuing this as much as I do. Without you, I would still be floating between my notes and my flash drive. You provide me with the anchor every writer needs.

Thank you, Randy—you spearhead the ever-echoing questions of accountability: Are you writing? How's the writing? Thank you for your friendship and for the premiere level of love and expectation you bring to this work. Your presence in my life makes me a better writer, and you make a huge difference for me. I'm ever-grateful.

Thank you, Annette, for the gift of our children. You are an extraordinary mother, and your loving heart speaks through their generosity, their freedom and their joy.

Tom McGuiness—for being the first professional to introduce me to his colleagues as My Writer. You changed my life on that day.

To four teachers who brought me the language and pushed me to make it my own: James Cross, Don Gaytan, Jean Weber and Stephen Cooper. Jean, I'll forever remember the lima beans in your nose.

To my brothers, Dennis and Mike, for being men I so easily respect, love and am impressed by. Mike—thank you for finding me in my dungeon and for pulling me out. And to my sisters, Teresa, Kath, Christine and Marie, for listening and for demanding more from me than my athleticism ever could. Dad—you are the forever imprint on my soul. Mom—you provide order, without which I don't even want to consider. Thank you—my young heart needed you.

So many have asked me when this collection would be published—and I'm grateful for all those reminders. Chip Royston, you pushed me over the cliff at the end. Thanks for getting me here.

Thank you, Melissa Foliente, for designing a cover for this book that so aptly represents what's inside. You listen, and you are a professional.

Also, to my cousin, Kimberly Wassenberg, for the beautiful photograph. You captured me walking with two people who are dear to me—my son, Luke, and my niece, Camille. Thank you for the joy and passion you bring to your photographic expertise.

And most especially, thank you to my children—Timarie, Jessi, Luke and Peter—for all your questions, for believing, for doubting, for your courage, your honesty and your willingness to face life head-on even when it's difficult. You each impress me.

Luke, thank you for allowing me to include *Coach Louie* here. I just read it again, and it's my favorite story of the bunch.

If you have any questions or comments regarding these stories or storytelling in general, please contact me at jon@WordsCreateWorlds.com.

For Timarie

CONTENTS

SHORT STORIES

Permission

My wife was out visiting with friends that night. I sat on the couch reading Rick Reilly's back-page article in this month's Sports Illustrated. Our five year old son, Patrick, played Nintendo in front of the TV. His older sister and brother kept to themselves somewhere in the house.

"DAD!" Our daughter, Rachel, yelled from her bedroom, "Can you get Kelsey out of my room?"

Like an uninvited stranger, Kelsey slithered down the hallway toward the living room. She paused a moment before entering. Her straight, black hair framed her face. Leaning against the wall, she stood just a bit taller than the television console.

We celebrated her fourth birthday two months ago. Her face looked older. Her sharp, black eyes cut across the room from Patrick at the TV to me on the couch; her petite body just a shadow in the hallway. Then, she entered and brushed her little hand along the couch cushions until she reached where I sat. She stopped, turned and surveyed the living room again.

She decided to join Patrick sitting on the floor in front of the television. She walked over, sat down, grabbed a controller and pushed reset.

"DAD!" Patrick turned to me. "She *can't* just do that!"

Breathing heavily, his big eyes pleaded with me, ready to explode.

"DAD? I was in the middle of a game. She *can't* just push reset without asking. That's not fair!"

By the time I weighed the validity of Patrick's complaint against his unwillingness to cut Kelsey some slack and include her in the game anyway, she dropped the controller and rolled away from him. She sat there looking at him, at the Nintendo apparatus, and then back at me—her lips pursed tight.

I picked up the magazine and continued reading.

Kelsey found some building blocks on the floor to fiddle with. She stacked up four or five of them, and then knocked them down. She spread the blocks in front of her. She looked at them with her mouth still closed, her expression hiding behind protective eyes.

She picked up a block and examined it. She picked up another block the same shape and color as the first. She put these two together in a pile, and added a third and a fourth to match. Slowly, methodically, she categorized the blocks. Eventually, she had the entire collection of blocks separated into eight piles, first by color and shape, and then by size. The yellows, reds and blues each had two piles, small and large. The orange and green blocks each had only one pile of the smaller ones.

She sat back on her heels looking at her organized piles, and her face relaxed.

When she came to live with us, Kelsey was a tiny, slight three and a half year old. Her Mom struggled with drug addictions. Unable to kick the habits and provide a stable home for Kelsey, her Mom asked us to take Kelsey while she attended a thirty-day lock-up program. That was eight months ago.

We treated Kelsey like one of our own children. But, away from her Mom and away from familiar habits and rhythms, ours was a strange culture for her. In our home, No meant No. For the first few weeks, Kelsey looked at us like she didn't understand the word No. We learned she was accustomed to dictating the rules—bedtime, meals and the rest.

In our home, she had the freedom to be a kid because the adults around her were parenting. Her whims did not rule the day. We loved her, and Kelsey struggled to share, listen and obey the rules. Sometimes stoic and defiant, sometimes she yelled, kicked and screamed. She didn't know how to be a friend. She found no bridge between her and the people in her life.

Rachel came down the hallway from her bedroom, entered the living room and saw Kelsey sitting with her piles of blocks.

"Hey, great Kelsey. Do you wanna build something?" She asked, already sitting down in front of Kelsey and handling a big yellow block.

"NO!" Kelsey blurted. "That's mine," and she reached out and grabbed the block away from Rachel.

"Fine." Rachel spun her body around on the floor and sat beside Patrick.

"What's her problem?" asked James, our nine year old son. He entered the living room pointing at Kelsey and sat down on the floor, on the other side of Patrick.

The three of them negotiated the next game: who got which controller, which character, which level, etc., and they pushed reset and began playing. With their backs toward Kelsey and I, their attention disappeared into the television screen.

Furious, Kelsey's little black eyes darkened further. She tightened her lips, and she stared at the backs of their heads. Then, she looked down at her blocks in their coordinated piles. Slowly and deliberately, she mixed up the colors and shapes. She left no discernable pattern among the blocks. They were now, again, merely a pile of assorted blocks on the floor.

After a moment, she turned and looked at me. I put the magazine down on the table in front of me and gave her my full attention. I waited for her to say something. She said nothing. She stared at me, her little body taut, her jaw jutting out and just barely shivering. Her steady and protected eyes gave no notice to the tremor she held still in her body—a complete system shut down.

Her practiced control concerned me. Everything about her surged, a volcano ready to spill over. Energy on fire, she and I were alone in the moment looking for answers. I wanted to be four again and yell for her—scream out how unfair it was that her Mom and Dad weren't around, that she'd probably never see her Dad, that I don't know if her damn Mom would ever recover enough to be her parent again. I wanted to explode for her, somehow give her the release of letting out all that she held so tight.

Why am I alone in someone else's home? Who are these people? I don't belong here! Why do I have to cope with this? Why don't I have a Dad? Why am I left out? Where's my Mom? She said she was just going to the doctor and she'd be back? Where the hell is she?

As an angry young child, I knew no such ability, as Kelsey did, to maintain any semblance of composure. I crawled out of my skin trying to reconcile within myself the inconsistencies of those around me. If I were Kelsey at her age, I'd have thrown the blocks across the room right at their heads. I'd run across the room and launch myself bodily at Patrick and the other kids. I'd disrupt every aspect of their Nintendo paradise until they no longer were capable of shutting me out. Someone (my older brother or my Dad) would have to peel me off them and drag me away to an empty room for my own safety as well as theirs.

At the very least, I'd be screaming, trembling and crying. As a young boy, I had no words, and certainly no ability to control the raging physical tremors. I hated myself for these episodes that consumed my body, and I hated the descriptions of me that followed—hyper, spastic, crazy—words my heart would contend with thereafter. I could see now the relief my family knew when the sport of football absorbed my passions.

Though Kelsey had many loud reactions during her stay with us, she most often exhibited the ability to keep her boiling anger inside—like a trained dog waiting at an invisible line until the master releases the hold. But until this particular evening, Kelsey knew no such permission.

She sat across the living room from me. Close to dinnertime, I thought I should get up and finish preparing our meal. Mesmerized by the intensity of her stare, I motioned for her to come over and sit on the couch beside me. She did so, slowly, dragging her composure with her. Instead of sitting, though, she stood there facing me.

"You're mad," I said to her.

She didn't respond. She looked down at the floor, away from me.

"It's okay to be mad, Kelsey."

Still no response—maybe a slight movement in her body.

"Kelsey, everybody gets mad. It might help if you yelled or something. Let it out."

No movement. Her demeanor settled into the silence she had mastered at her young age. The more I tried to draw her out, the more something held her in place, entrenched.

"Kelsey, did someone tell you it's not okay to be mad?"

Her black eyes shot right up to me, and she unveiled a small corner. I could see I'd hit the mark. After that brief moment of recognition, though, the whites of her eyes dimmed, and she lowered her head again.

"Maybe," I said, "if you hit a pillow or something, you'd feel better."

She looked up at me, her body unmoving. I thought if I touched her, she'd fall over, dissipate and fade away.

"See, here," I said. I turned my body around to face the couch cushions behind me. I fluffed one up and placed it directly in front of me. Then, I balled up a fist and hit the pillow with a soft blow.

"Now, you do it," I said, moving aside to allow her ample space.

She looked at me and tilted her head, like I spoke a language foreign to her. Then, she leaned her leg against the couch and collapsed her entire tiny torso onto the cushions, her face sideways staring up at me.

"You don't have to hit it if you don't want to. But, you can kick it. You can jump on it. Anything. When you move your body, sometimes, you can get your anger out, and it doesn't feel so bad inside."

She didn't move. Limp on the couch, she stared now into space.

I noticed James had abandoned Nintendo. He leaned back watching us. He looked at me. His eyes were questioning. He seemed to be asking, "Shouldn't we just leave her alone?"

Rachel turned toward us.

"Kelsey, it really does work," she said. "Just hit it. You'll feel better."

"Kelsey!" Patrick said, "Watch!"

Patrick jumped up from his Nintendo game and darted over to the couch. Kelsey moved away to allow him access to the couch cushions.

Bam, Bam, Bam. He punched the couch with fervor. Bam, Bam, Bam. He punched the couch again.

"See. I feel great," Patrick proclaimed, and he ran back to his spot on the floor, picked up his controller and resumed his game.

I slid across the couch until I sat next to Kelsey, and then I knelt on the floor beside her. My torso was the size of her whole body, head to toe. I put out my hand, palm up, (like a tennis racket next to her), and she laid her flat palm on top of mine. She looked at our hands for a moment and then looked up into my eyes.

"Did your Mom tell you not to ever be mad?"

Holding our stare, her little head nodded just slightly. Her straight, black hair barely moved as she allowed this revelation.

"It's hard, though, huh?"

She kept nodding, and her deep eyes began to well.

I looked into her eyes, and I told her, "Kelsey, you're living with us now, in our home. And for now, this is your home. And while you're living with us, I want you to know it's okay to be mad. In fact, I don't think we can help it. Sometimes we just get mad. You almost can't control it.

"But we can control the way we handle it. And it's hard on your body if you keep it in there."

I put my other palm out on her solar plexus.

"Isn't it?"

She nodded, and I reached up to wipe the one tear that fell out of her eye and escaped down her cheek.

"So, sometimes it helps us to just get it out. And I'm telling you it's okay to hit our couch when you're mad. When you're mad, you can hit our couch however you want. Hit it. Kick it. I don't care. Just get it out. And I won't get mad at you. I won't get mad if you hit the couch. Just do it whenever you want."

She made no further expression. She faced me but showed no recognition. For something this simple, she had so many things to consider.

"Kelsey," I said, leaning forward, "I love you—no matter what. If you want to hit the couch, fine. And you don't *ever* have to hit the couch if you don't want to. I love you whether you hit it or not."

No expression.

"I'm going into the kitchen now and get dinner ready," I told her. I got up from the floor, fluffed her hair and went into the kitchen. Kelsey stood alone near the couch. Rachel, James and Patrick began another video game.

A few minutes into dinner preparations, I leaned my head around the wall to check on Kelsey. She had climbed up onto the couch and, lying there on her back looking up to the ceiling, she was tiny. Only her feet and her head stretched longer than the length of the middle cushion. She looked like a big, beautiful insect, belly up. I went back to making dinner.

Minutes later, I heard a sound I couldn't decipher. Thud. Soft and low. Thud. Thud. Thud.

I peaked around the wall again and saw Kelsey kicking the couch cushion. From her lying down position, she cautiously extended her leg and deliberately pounded her heel down on the cushion.

Rachel looked at me, surprised and smiling. Kelsey didn't notice us.

I finished dinner and set out the dishes and the forks. I pulled the baked potatoes from the oven. All the while, Kelsey's slow, methodical thudding continued.

Almost ready to call the kids to the table, I walked into the living room and stood beside Kelsey on the couch. She looked up at me and released an innocent smile. I smiled back at her.

"That's great," I said. "Let it out."

Her leg stopped.

"Go ahead. Make a good grunt when you kick it. You'll feel better."

No movement.

By calling attention to her kicking, she had again decided to withdraw. James was probably right. Maybe I should just leave her alone.

"Come on. Turn off the Nintendo. Let's go. Wash your hands. Dinner's ready."

My kids were hungry, so they jumped up and marched into the bathroom to wash. I returned to the kitchen, opened the refrigerator and grabbed the butter and the milk.

Bam, Bam, Bam. That unmistakable sound. Bam, Bam, Bam. Bam, Bam, Bam. Patrick must be showing Kelsey again. Bam, Bam, Bam. Bam, Bam, Bam. But I looked across the living room and all three of my kids stood still in the hallway, having just come from washing their hands in the bathroom.

Bam, Bam, Bam. Grunt, huff, puff. Bam, Bam, Bam. They were watching Kelsey. I turned to see her. Bam, Bam, Bam. Huff, puff. Bam, Bam, Bam.

She stood, facing the couch and throwing punch after punch after punch after punch. Throwing her small body into every thrust. Letting out her exaggerated Karate-chop grunt with each blow, she was relentless, lost in the action.

"Go, Kelsey, Go!" Patrick shouted.

Rachel threw her hands in the air and hooted and hollered.

James looked at me, and we both smiled and nodded our heads.

After many minutes, Kelsey turned and faced the room. She sat on the couch, her hands flat on the cushions to each side of her, and she sighed a heavy breath. She held her chin high, and she smiled. We all paused for a moment and looked at one another.

Then, Kelsey popped up and whirled around and began again to pound the couch. Bam, Bam, Bam. Bam, Bam, Bam. Every fifth punch or so, she wound up a big one and slammed down a pronounced thud. I could see her smiling, and the sound she grunted sounded like laughter. The other kids and I stood there and let her go. We didn't dare move, catch her attention or interrupt her in any way. She just kept going. Bam, bam, bam. Her energy ran at a steady pace. Bam, bam, bam. She lunged her small body at the couch and bounced backward. She jumped toward the couch again and continued her barrage of punches. She punched and punched and punched.

I had goose bumps on my arms. Kelsey was emerging, and her life would never be the same. Like watching *Rocky* for the first time, or *Shawshank Redemption*—a triumph of the human spirit. I looked across the room, glad my kids were here for this.

Kelsey paused, breathing and heaving and smiling, her arms dangling in front of her. *What now?* Kelsey looked around at each of us. She seemed to be asking, *Where do I go from here?*

Rachel said, "Come in here and pound on your bed," and she disappeared down the hall into her bedroom to Kelsey's bed. Kelsey followed her and jumped on the bed and began punching.

Patrick, James and I stood in their bedroom doorway and watched. With renewed focus, Kelsey threw everything she had into that bed. She pounded her punches. She bounced on her knees, slamming down her fists. She leaned back and kicked her heels into the pillow. She turned back around and threw more punches.

When Kelsey finished, she laid her head down on the bed, breathing. Rachel rubbed her back softly and asked, "Do you feel better?"

"Yes!" Kelsey whispered her exclamation. Her eyes brightened, and she smiled. Her straight, black hair glistened.

"Do you wanna come to dinner?" Rachel asked.

"Yes!" Together we walked through the living room and into the kitchen to our dining table nestled in the nook.

Patrick, James and Rachel devoured their meal, and Kelsey picked at her food and ate nothing. She said nothing. Halfway through dinner, she closed her eyes. She laid her head down on the table, and her glimmering black hair fell into her plate. I picked her limp, sweaty body up into my arms and carried her off to bed. She didn't stir when I put her down. I brushed her hair out of her face and kissed her forehead.

The 5K

Patrick slumped in the chair at the computer desk, barely looking over the keyboard tray, poking at the keys—disinterested in the video game battle raging onscreen; his resident intensity for computer games temporarily on vacation.

"What's wrong, Patrick?"

"Why can't I go to the gym?"

"Well, you're not twelve. They won't let you in."

"I'll *never* get to go."

The game continued. The view of the battlefield shifted left to right, showing a straight shot at the formerly undercover bad guy. Patrick glanced at the screen and chose to ignore the opportunity. The bad guy lifted his weapon and aimed at Patrick's character.

"I can't even go jogging around the block."

At this point, I recognized he was talking about something other than the fact that I'd just driven his older brother and sister to the gym. I dropped them off and came home to prepare dinner.

"Why can't you go jogging?" I asked him.

"Without Pooca?" He looked over to me, his eyes rolling back. His body slid lower in the chair.

Well, of course, I thought. You're eight years old. You're not just running out into the world without supervision or protection. What if you never came back? I couldn't live with that.

"Pooca slows me down, Dad." He looked right at me.

What's he getting at?

"She doesn't run straight. And her leash gets wrapped around my legs. And she stops all the time to smell everything. And then she poops on all the lawns."

What's he getting at? He's eight years old. Since when is Patrick so interested in jogging and exercise. He's athletic enough, I thought, but something else is bugging him.

I let it go and turned toward the refrigerator to get the leftovers and heat them up. Why does Patrick want to go running? Why all of a sudden are my older kids at the gym and my youngest wants to go jogging?

I turned toward Patrick still slumped at the computer.

The 5K. He wants to prepare for his school's 5K Run. Oh, yeah. Okay. Now, I get it.

"Patrick?" I asked him. "You want me to take you jogging?"

"Yeah, let's go." He stood up and then darted down the hallway to his room to get his shoes.

"Hey, Patrick," I yelled down the hall. "I'm just going to ride the bike while you run. Okay?"

I didn't want to run. I didn't even want to go out. I looked down at my dress shoes and slacks. I didn't want to change my clothes. I was tired from my day at work and just wanted to get dinner going.

"Let's go, Dad."

Patrick stood in front of me ready to go, the laces on his shoes already tied. He bounced on his toes, reached over, grabbed my hand and pulled me toward the front door. I didn't want to go.

I rolled the bicycle down the driveway and into the street. Patrick followed.

"Are you running in the street?"

He shrugged his shoulders and turned up the street and proceeded to run beside me on the black asphalt. And he ran. I was glad not to be jogging with him. I couldn't have kept up. I pedaled a little and then rolled along. Patrick ran.

About halfway down the block he stopped for something. I couldn't tell for what exactly, but I thought he must be tired. He abruptly reached down for his belt buckle, unhooked it, lifted up his pants, and cinched his belt even tighter. Then, he took off running again in the same direction.

He had long pants on. Why don't my kids wear shorts to work out in? I don't get it. Patrick's running in a pair of jeans, and they're long around his ankles. His t-shirt is baggy and swaying with his stride.

The next street was coming up, and I thought he'd want to turn right and take the shorter route around the block.

"Are you turning here?" I asked.

He pointed past this corner to up ahead where the street ended into a cross street. When we got there, he turned right. We passed a few homes of people we knew. Two girls played basketball in their driveway, and they stopped momentarily to watch Patrick run. This was the longest street in the tract and much further away from our home than I expected Patrick to go. That's the problem with going jogging. In addition to the distance you run away from home, there's always the fuel efficiency issue of getting back. There's that point when far enough becomes too far.

We just kept going.

A car approached us from the other direction. The driver slowed down. She leaned forward over her steering wheel and smiled as Patrick passed by.

I looked over and saw Patrick running hard. His face scrunched up and wincing, he sucked in each breath as if unsure of the oxygen. The shoes on his growing feet slapped the asphalt. Riding the bike alongside, watching him, listening to his breathing, I wondered when he'd start walking.

But he took the next street right and began the zig-zag among the shorter streets that took us back to the final stretch down our long street home. And his pace continued. The breathing. The footsteps. The staccato rhythm. His face focused on the road in front of him.

"Patrick, you're doing great," I said to him.

We still had a long way to go, and he ran with unquestionable determination. I became concerned that he would hyperventilate.

"Patrick, you're really doing great. Concentrate on your breathing. As you run, try to breathe slower and more relaxed. Relax your breathing."

Instantly, his breathing quieted.

"That's it. In. Out. In. Out. Slow like that. And you'll be able to run longer. You don't want your breathing to tire you out. You want all your energy in your legs."

He turned right and surprised me. I was in his way. I hadn't seen the street. My bike blocked his pathway. He looked annoyed.

Pointing in the direction he wanted to go, he said, "This way", and he side-stepped, let me pass and veered around me into the last long corner before our street.

"Look up. Run with your head up. You want to see as far in front of you as you can. Looking down slows you down."

He turned at our street. Every part of him in sync, he was a runner. His commitment made his baggy jeans look appropriate. At eight-years-old, Patrick confidently pushed into an unknown region of himself.

"Keep going. You're doing great."

He wasn't slowing down.

"Awesome, Patrick!"

I looked down the long street and worried about the remaining distance from home. I wondered if he'd slow down before we got there. But, his pace continued. Rhythmic. His face showed a certainty of purpose. Though the pain from the long haul started to sway his shoulders, he pulled for the finish. This was Patrick beside me, and I remember feeling proud riding beside him and watching him push himself—determined to prepare for the school's 5K Run that was two weeks out. He wanted to win that race. In the third grade now, Patrick would be running with the older grades. In grades K, 1 and 2, he ran an abbreviated course, and I remembered now how important it was for him to do his best—and to win.

It wasn't likely he'd win the race this year. He would be competing with students in grades 4 and 5. I tried to think of the kids I knew in those grades, wondering whether they were training like this. Not likely. I looked up and saw we were about forty yards from home.

"Patrick?" I said, pedaling next to him. "You're doing great. Keep going."

He wasn't about to slow down now. He was making it all the way.

"You know how at the end of the 5K . . ." I waited a moment. "How do you finish the race?"

I paused.

"At the very end, how do you finish the race?"

He didn't look over at me. He didn't say a word. But somehow, he picked up his pace. His legs reached further in front of him. He got taller, faster.

"That's it, Patrick! Take it home! Keep going! All the way!"

I couldn't believe it. His resolve and determination were exhilarating. Patrick ran all the way down the street.

At our driveway, he went up the curb onto the front lawn where he abruptly stopped, bent over and threw up everything in his young stomach. When he finally stood up, he wiped his mouth on the front of his shirt. He walked once around the lawn and went in the front door.

Patrick and Daniel

Loud heaving and uncontrolled grief. I couldn't recognize who it was, but this grieving sound reminded me of the gasping that escaped my Grandmother as she collapsed outside the church after my Uncle's funeral. Pure and guttural, this noise now came from the other side of my home-office wall.

The familiar sounds around the house were still there. The water ran in the kitchen. I assumed my wife, Sara, was either doing the dishes or preparing dinner. The echoes from our backyard pool drifted in through my open window. Our kids ran and splashed with their friends, playing some game of hide-and-dive in the deep end. The chimes hanging from our eaves swung in the afternoon breeze.

I hadn't heard this sad sound in my home before, though. Concerned that a neighborhood kid was hurt and no one was responding, I got up from my computer, went out of my office and turned right toward our front door.

There on the floor in the hallway was our youngest son, five year old Patrick, balled up tightly and crying a fierce and painful sorrow. Immediately, I bent down to check him out. I rolled him over on the floor looking for blood. No blood. So, I wrapped my arms around him to gather him into my embrace.

He pushed my comfort away, reached down for the floor to be left alone. This was private. He didn't want me to alleviate even an ounce of the hurt.

I looked down at him for a moment. His self-awareness surprised me. Why would he want to feel the pain?

I walked into the kitchen.

"Sara," I asked. "What happened to Patrick?"

"Yeah," she said, wiping her hands on a small towel and turning toward me. We both stood there listening to the sad sound of Patrick in the hallway.

"He was making fun of Daniel," she continued, "and Daniel went home."

"Daniel's in eighth grade," I thought aloud. "Patrick's in kindergarten."

"They were playing Nintendo like they always do," she explained. "Daniel is always so good with Patrick. But Patrick was making fun of Daniel's acne, and he didn't realize how upset Daniel was. Daniel asked him to stop, but he kept laughing and digging. Daniel finally asked Patrick if he wanted him to leave. Patrick kept laughing and pointing at his face. So, Daniel got up and left."

"He wouldn't let me pick him up," I said. "He really wants to feel it."

"He's sad. He thinks Daniel will *never* come back. He told me he lost his best friend today."

We stood there in the kitchen and noticed Patrick's loud grief subsiding into a low, weeping cry.

"Let me get dinner going," she said.

I walked into the living room and sat on the couch. I could see Patrick from there. I looked for a magazine on the coffee table and held it open on my lap so Patrick wouldn't think I was staring at him. After a time, he sat up in the hallway on the tile floor. He caught his breath. Then, he stood up and came into the living room and sat beside me on the couch.

Slumped over into the throw pillows, he didn't look at me. He struggled to compose himself, wiping his dribbling nose on his sleeve.

I asked him, "Something bad happen?"

"Yeah."

"What happened?"

Silence.

"You alright?"

"No," he whispered.

"Do you want to talk about it?"

"No."

I patted him on the knee, got up from the couch, and stepped past him and over toward the kitchen. I saw through the kitchen window that the summer sun still had over an hour or so. I looked around the kitchen and saw Sara working on some elaborate, multi-process meal. The table had two plates of chopped and diced, and the grated was on the counter near the sink. The oven behind me was preheating.

"Mind if I take Patrick to the park?"

"Good luck." She turned toward me, "I doubt he'll want to go."

"We won't be long."

"No problem," she said. "I've got to run to the store for Soy Sauce, anyway. Dinner won't be until later."

I walked past Patrick and reached into the hall closet for a small football, a soft one that fit into my palm. I then went into my bedroom for socks and shoes, and I returned to the couch to put my shoes on. I set the ball on the table.

As I tied my second shoe, Patrick rolled toward me and asked, "Where you going?"

"I'm thinking of walking over to the park."

I finished my shoes and sat there. Then, I picked up the ball and leaned back away from him. I showed him the ball, and he put his hands up for the catch. He caught it and threw it back to me. We tossed it back and forth, back and forth.

"You want to go with me?"

He nodded, and he leaned over and reached his arms out for me.

"Should we bring the ball?"

He shook his head. I left the ball on the table and stood up. His body slumped and rested against my chest. I looked to Sara in the kitchen, and we headed for the door.

Once outside, he sat up in my arms a little more restless, looking around as I walked down the driveway and into the street.

"Want to sit on my shoulders?" I asked.

"Yeah."

I turned his body facing forward and set my hands under his arms. Then, I lifted him high up over my head and onto his perch on my shoulders. He shifted until we both were satisfied with his position. I walked in silence around the block, and we reached the park entrance.

"What happened with Daniel?"

"He went home."

"What happened?"

"I was pointing at the red dots on his face and laughing and he said to me to stop it and I just kept laughing."

"Then, what happened?"

"He said he was going to go home if I didn't stop laughing."

I stopped at a bench in the tall grass surrounded by three shade trees. I maneuvered Patrick off my shoulders and set him on the bench. Then, I sat down beside him. I stayed quiet. The sun squatted into the horizon, splashing bits of red streaking clouds to either side. The yellow-orange sky began to fade.

"Dad?"

"Yeah?"

"I don't think Daniel wants to be my friend anymore."

"Do you know why?"

"I was mean."

I started slowly, "Well, Patrick, you injured the relationship."

"What's *the relationship?*"

"The relationship between you and Daniel."

"But . . ." He thought for a moment. "What *is* a relationship?"

Good question. How do I explain that to him? I never thought of a relationship as an explainable thing. I just knew how I felt about others. Some relationships were good and healthy, and some were awkward and frustrating.

"It's the nature of things between you and someone else." I thought for a moment. "It's like with you and me. I'm your Dad, and you're my Son. And between us we have this Dad/Son relationship. Some relationships are with friends and family. And I have business relationships."

"Dad?"

"Yeah?"

"Can a relationship be a bad thing?"

"It can be a difficult thing. Like with someone you don't get along with. Or with someone who doesn't like you or who is mean to you."

"What do you mean by *injured the relationship?*"

"You hurt it. When you hurt Daniel, he left. You injured the relationship by not caring how Daniel was feeling."

"But, I *do* care how Daniel feels."

That's a bad place to be, (I thought of my own relationships), when you want someone to know something but you're sure they won't believe you or even listen to you.

"Does Daniel know that?"

Silence.

I looked over to Patrick and saw him sniffling a new cry. Then, I put my arm around him and pulled him in close to me. He relaxed into my side, okay with the comfort now.

"We all make mistakes, Patrick."

Silence.

"It's not what you did that's important."

He turned his head up toward me with a big questioning look on his face.

"The important part is what you do now."

"What could I do if Daniel doesn't want to be my friend?"

He sat up and looked at me with some new possibility in his eyes. His expectation made me nervous.

"Well, you could heal the relationship."

"How do you heal the relationship?" Another good question.

"There are a lot of ways," I said without certainty. I hoped I could think of a few ways. "I think if you let Daniel know how important your relationship with him is to you, and that you realized after he left that you hurt him. I think you could tell him how sad you are thinking you hurt him, and you want to be his friend."

I wondered if my explanation satisfied him.

"Patrick," I said, "I think if you told him you were sorry, it would help to heal your relationship."

"Yeah," he stood up. "I could do that."

He started walking toward the neighborhood. I walked up next to him and put my hand out. He grabbed it. We walked through the park's gate, down the street and to the corner.

"You want a shoulder ride?"

"Yeah."

I bent down, then, and looked into his eyes.

"You know, Patrick. The fastest way to heal your relationship is to talk to Daniel. And I bet he'd like that. I bet he's sad now, too." I paused for a moment, and Patrick thought about that.

"We could walk over to Daniel's house," I continued. "I bet he'd be happy to see you."

"Yeah," he said without hesitation. He nodded his head, "Let's go."

I lifted him up into the air and onto my shoulders. Instead of turning left toward our house, I crossed over two streets and down Daniel's block.

"Dad?"

"Yeah?"

"What do I say to Daniel?" Perhaps the best question so far. What should he say? What do you say when you're sad and lonely and you're not sure you can say anything that would make a difference?

"You just tell him what you told me. That you *do* care how he feels. That your relationship with him *is* important to you. And that you're sorry for hurting the relationship by making fun of him."

I thought for a moment. Then, I continued, "That's it really. You see? Daniel's on the other side of your relationship. You admit where you messed up, you say you're sorry, and you let him say whatever he has to say. He might have some things he wants to say to you."

About three houses down from Daniel's, I lifted Patrick off my shoulders and set him on his feet on the sidewalk. I bent down to prepare him.

"The most important thing to do is to be honest with him, and to apologize for your behavior. He'll understand. Daniel really likes you, Patrick. And this is important to him, too." I put my hand out palm up, and Patrick laid his palm on mine. He nodded his head ready to go, and we walked over to their driveway and up to the door.

I knocked on the door and waited.

"Hey, come on in," Daniel's Dad opened the door. "Hi, Patrick. How you doing?"

We both looked down and saw only the top of Patrick's head. I stepped into the doorway and spoke quietly.

"We're here because Patrick wants to talk with Daniel. He has something he wants to say."

"Oh, sure, come on in." Daniel's Dad understood the nature of the situation.

I followed him into the house to the living room. Their family was scattered about: in front of the television, preparing food in the kitchen, and Daniel played computer games sitting at the desk. Daniel turned toward me, and I turned toward Patrick. Patrick wasn't next to me, though. He stood outside on the porch with his head down.

"Patrick wanted to talk to you," I said to Daniel.

Daniel smiled and immediately stood up. He walked past me and out to Patrick. He bent over and put his arm around Patrick's shoulders. Patrick began talking, and Daniel's head nodded up and down a few times. Then, it was over.

They walked into the house together past me, and Daniel sat down to continue his computer game. Patrick stood next to Daniel's chair and watched the game. He lifted his arm and rested his elbow on Daniel's shoulder.

I turned to Daniel's Dad, and we both smiled and nodded our heads. We discussed a few things about the school and our families, but mainly we kept looking back to Daniel and Patrick. After a while, it was time to go. The sun was almost down. Dinner would be ready.

"Patrick, let's go."

Patrick and Daniel shook hands, and Daniel returned to his game.

We said goodbye and walked out the door holding hands. When we got to the sidewalk, Patrick turned toward me and reached his arms up. I hoisted him onto my shoulders and headed home.

"That's a big thing you did."

"What do you mean?"

"You healed your relationship." I didn't want to say too much. "I'm proud of you, Patrick. It takes a lot of courage to do that. That's a big thing."

We walked on.

When we turned the corner to our street, my wife drove past us in our van, returning from the store. She waved and pulled into the driveway. She didn't get out. She rolled down her window and waited for us.

I took Patrick off my shoulders, and we walked up beside the van.

"Where have you boys been?"

"Mom," Patrick stood on his tippy-toes against the van door, his voice rising, "I was healing my relationship with Daniel." He lingered and looked into his Mom's glistening eyes with triumphant joy.

The Good Night

James was in his bed with lights out when I arrived home from work. At four years old, 9pm was past his bedtime, but he'd been waiting to see me. I bent down into the lower bunk. He smiled.

"Hi, Dad."

"Hey, Champ."

He smiled, and I lowered myself the remaining distance to the bedroom floor and kneeled down to be with him. I reached over and moved the hair back from his forehead, and I caressed his face. His eyes softened sleepily.

"How was your day today?" I asked.

"I had a *great* day today, Dad," he responded to me. His smile broadened, and he looked into my eyes.

"How was *your* day today?" he asked me.

"I had a pretty crappy day," I said.

The words came out of my mouth, and I regretted them. *Crap* was still uncommon enough in the lexicon of our home to be shocking to him, and here I dropped it carelessly. The vile and venomous residue from my day at work still coursed through my veins. Here in front of me the face of love and appreciation awaited my arrival, and yet I allowed the tide of resignation to take me elsewhere. I thought of this, kneeling there in front of my son. I didn't like myself much.

I brushed his hair back and tried again, "But, you know James, when I come home and see you, I'm reminded of how great my life is and how lucky I am to be your Dad."

"You know, Dad," he said, "I feel the same way when I see you."

I heard what he said, but I couldn't accept the gift he offered. I squinted in the dark, took a long, deep breath and looked at this beautiful boy in front of me. He didn't know how ugly I felt inside. He simply smiled and looked into my eyes.

I looked away to the wall, then to the ceiling and around the dark room. So much in my life was not how I wanted it. I made poor decisions in my business. I didn't know how to do it. I was embarrassed at the tight spots I'd gotten into and, especially, of the difficult financial squeeze my wife endured. Today, the IRS called, and I spoke to an agent who didn't care much about my problems. She wanted to confirm my next payment, and I couldn't offer her any assurance. I was three months behind on the mortgage. They weren't going to wait indefinitely. I didn't want to go out into the living room and read the list of phone messages from creditors.

Amongst all this, the presence of my children humbled me. I couldn't possibly deserve so pure a love. The undertow pulled at me. The ugliness took over, and more words came out.

"James," I stared. "People make mistakes." I looked at him as he listened to me.

He lifted his little hand up to my face and caressed my cheek.

"Well, Dad," he whispered, "I've never seen you make *one*."

He smiled softly. He lowered his hand down next to his little body. His eyes faded, and he was off to sleep. I wiped the tears from my eyes, leaned forward and kissed him on the cheek. I touched his forehead, hesitated, and stood up. I walked out of the dark room.

The Craw

I arrived home from work to James' bobbing, bouncing head.

"Come on, Dad. Let's wrestle," James said, running from the living room to meet me in the entryway. He grabbed my arm above the elbow, pulled lightly and then squeezed with both hands. As his grip tightened, he lifted his feet off the ground, suspending his three year old body by dangling on my arm.

"Yeah, Dad. Can we wrestle?" asked Rachel.

"Hang on," I said backing up, concerned that five year old Rachel would also jump on. Carrying them both on one arm was too much.

"I am hanging on," James dropped his head backward to swing all his weight from my arm. I bent down to my left, lowering him until his curled-up feet rested on the ground.

"Up, up, up," he yelled. "Come on, Dad! Lift me up! Swing me! Let's wrestle."

I looked at James hanging there, and then at Rachel. Her eyes wanted permission. I got the sense they had waited all afternoon, anticipating when I'd walk through the door.

"Okay, okay," I said. "Give me a minute first, though."

I caught James' gaze, and he stopped swinging. I think he merely expected me to say No. How many times had they asked and pleaded recently, only to have me refuse, too tired from the day at work? We used to have a daily wrestle.

He reached his toes down to the tile floor and let his grip go.

"Give me just a second to put my laptop away and to get dressed."

"Yeah, Dad. We'll wait. But hurry up, okay." Rachel's eyes pleaded. "You always say that," she reminded me.

"Okay, I'll be really quick."

I moved forward into the living room and hurried down the hall through the bedroom door. First, I put the laptop case down on the bed. Then, I loosened and untied my tie. I unbuttoned my dress shirt, tossed it on the bed and unbuckled my pants. I found a pair of loose-fitting pajama pants and headed out toward the living room. I lifted my head and saw the kids.

They froze. Like characters in a wax museum, they stood poised. They waited side by side, each in the guarding position I taught them: left foot forward, right foot back, hands up and ready for battle. Across the room, waiting for the showdown to begin, this was the moment they wanted. They loved wrestling with me. I lowered, slowly, down to my knees.

Behind their stern seriousness and furrowed brows, slow grins emerged. Their faces lit up. First, James got antsy, swaying back and forth. Then, Rachel's giddiness gave way to a huge smile.

James let loose the first battle cry and ran the full length of the room. From his last step, he launched himself up and I bent my head down to the floor and he landed with his torso on the back of my neck. Like a crane, I lifted my head. His small, bare feet dangled in front of my eyes. He pounded his small fists on my lower back. I heard his howling enjoyment.

Rachel crept slowly in. She jumped up onto the couch next to me. I lifted myself up onto my knees, and James slid down behind me, falling onto my calves. In the next moment, Rachel flung herself out with her arms wide-open. She grabbed my neck, landing heavier than James, and I swayed on impact.

Let the games begin!

I pried Rachel's grip loose and pushed her away. When I turned to grab James, Rachel came back at me from a running start and thudded into me. She pushed me back further than I wanted to go. I caught James' shirt from the back and cinched up a handful of cloth in my hand. I lifted him up and swung him forward toward where Rachel sprawled on her back in a heap of laughter after bouncing off me. I set James softly down on top of his sister. They rolled off each other and hopped up into their guarding positions, ready for more.

James walked to my right, step by step, and Rachel circled to my left. They kept moving to my sides and then behind me.

I waited.

Five. Four. Three. Two.

Wham!

They both slammed against my back. James continued to climb up my leg and over my shoulder, bounding forward onto my lap. Rachel wrapped her arms around my neck and pulled backwards. I reached back and put my hand under her armpit and lifted her up over my shoulder spinning her headfirst, then landing her softly in front of me and pushing her up against James. She wobbled off balance and fell into his side.

Inexhaustible, the dance continued.

Each time I pushed them away, they raced back for more. The noise level rolled with grunts and howling laughter and deep breathing and the occasional screaming, "Dad!"

"Me! Dad!"

"Here I come, Dad!"

"Catch me, Dad!"

"My turn, Dad!"

"Me, Dad!"

On my back, I held them off from either side. They each battled an arm, fighting full out to control me, to stop my progress, to hold back the tide of my strength. They pulled my fingers and kneed my wrist and twisted my arm around—struggling to wrangle me into a pretzel.

I looked over to the kitchen and saw my wife, Sara, leaning up against the counter holding a tall glass of ice water. She smiled at me, enjoying the show. I guessed she'd been watching the whole time.

From the kitchen table, I heard a chair pull out. Rene crossed in front of Sara and entered the living room. Wearing shorts, her knobby knees walked on over. Rene smiled at me and stepped over my face on her way beside the couch through the living room to her bedroom. Without looking back, her bedroom door closed at the end of the hall.

Thirteen years old now, Rene was only five when we met. I dated Sara, her mother, for a few months, and Sara had been careful to keep me away.

I saw Rene the first time one night after a date. Sara's roommate babysat so we could go out. We came into the apartment after midnight and thought Rene was asleep. But she appeared from their room as soon as Sara got home. Rene rubbed her eyes in the hallway and walked directly to Sara and stood beside her Mom looking at me. At the time, I was mindless of this child's concerns. I approached Sara to embrace her goodnight, and Rene moved between the two of us. She remained wedged there and pushed me away.

Now, eight years later, this same child sat alone at the end of the hallway in our home. I tried to continue with the little ones, but something about her isolation in her room down the hall drew my attention to Rene.

I looked over at Rachel and James. I thought of their freedom and willingness to bound into me from a full run and how they could fly off the couch into the air knowing with absolute certainty that I would catch them. They were fearless with me. Like a bear, I pawed at them around the room, and they rolled and laughed and loved the aggression and safety they got from their Dad. They were eager for it.

I remembered my own Dad from when I was young. My Dad often lay down on our living room floor and watched football on the television. His head propped up on a large throw pillow, he sprawled with his arms stretched to each side. Sometimes, I'd lie down next to him, resting into his chest.

Out of the corner of my eye, I caught a movement. His hand stopped. He watched TV, and I watched his hand. It moved and stopped. The fingers extended outward, prone and poised. I was trapped. The hand dragged itself across the top of the carpet toward me. Fear and excitement came with it. My heart pounded. My eyes rounded, anticipating the huge fingers and the big, strong, powerful hand.

And then it was on me. His arm around my shoulders, the fingers tickled my ribs. I jumped and shifted and fought to get free.

"Dad. Daaaaad. DAAAAAD!" My voice escalated, and I jolted back and forth like a jumping bean.

Wiggle, wiggle, wiggle. I slipped free and rolled away across the room to catch my breath.

"Dad?!"

He stared blankly, uninterrupted, at the game.

"Dad!!!"

"Huh? What?" He looked over at me, blank face.

"*You know*, Dad. Come on?"

"What is it, Son?" he asked, overly concerned.

"Your hand!"

He looked down to his hand outstretched toward me. He pinched his eyebrows together like he didn't understand. He looked at me. I leaned back out of his reach, and I caught a movement. His hand stiffened. I steadied myself.

"You mean that?" he asked.

I nodded my head up and down.

"Be careful, Son," he warned me. "That's THE CRAW." He announced it with emphasis, like trying to be clear with a mouth full of peanut butter in his teeth, and his tongue got caught.

"NO!" I yelled. "Not THE CRAW!"

I sprang from my position up onto his forearm. I turned in mid-air so that I'd be between him and The Craw. I needed him there to support me. The Craw kept coming. No matter how often I slammed it back down on the carpet, The Craw always came back for more.

Both my little hands grabbed at the huge fingers. Like grabbing a bunch of bananas, I pulled and twisted. I rolled onto my back with both hands yanking on one finger. It bent a little, but soon would no longer budge. I rolled over on top of The Craw again and squeezed the wrist tight to cut off the blood.

The Craw gripped me and lifted me up into the air. My legs dangled, and I hung on, wrapped my arms around it to keep from slipping around and falling off.

"Dad, Dad, Dad!" I looked over to his face, and he stared blankly at the football game.

"Dad? Help me! It's THE CRAW!"

Slowly, the arm rested down on the ground and went limp, and The Craw disappeared. I rolled away, breathing and eyes poised for the action to begin again. Like a puppy, I played then ran away and now wanted to come back and play again.

"Dad!?"

"What?"

"The Craw!"

"What about it?"

"*You know!!*"

"Know what?" He asked innocently. "Come on over here and join me."

He patted the carpet with his hand, and I crawled over to him cautiously and curled up beside him. He wrapped his arm around me softly and cupped my shoulder with his hand. We went back to watching the game.

Lying there now on my own living room floor, I thought about the power and the force I experienced in my father's hands. With James on one side of me and Rachel on the other, I began to appreciate the value of their freedom and the gift my own Dad had been to me. I was a rag-doll compared to the strength of The Craw. He ruled the Law of Gravity. The strength was his, but I reveled in the comfort of knowing he'd never hurt me. He loved me, and I was safe with him.

Many of the risks I had taken in my teens and twenties came from my knowing the safety, love and guidance from his enormous hands. I could now see the beginnings of that courage and faith and security germinate in the play between my kids and me. Like a slow motion realization, they danced into their future, wrestling away the seeds of insecurity.

I looked down the hallway toward Rene's bedroom door. Shut. She was on the other side. In the eight years I'd known her, we never really wrestled. I realized while I lie there on the floor that she hadn't had the experience of being tossed with childish freedom. Without fear. No protection necessary. Caution cast to the wind. Knowing her Dad would catch her.

She hadn't lived with her father, ever, as a young child.

I was Dad now. But, I hadn't found a way through the calculated barriers this child packed up and brought with her when her Mom and I married and she began to live with a man called Dad. I considered this my responsibility.

Rachel and James startled when I quickly sat up and pulled them in close.

"Hey, you guys. Listen up," I said quietly to them. "Don't you think Rene ought to be out here?"

They shook their heads, and their eyes lit up.

"Now," I said, and they leaned in, listening intently to the scheme. "I'm going to go into Rene's room. Give me a minute to get her out here."

"She won't come out here, Dad," Rachel said.

"I'll carry her out."

James nodded his head up and down, liking the plan. Rachel wasn't so sure.

"She won't want to."

"Look. Do you want her out here or not?"

Rachel looked at me. She wasn't so sure I could talk Rene out of her bedroom.

"Go tell Mom," I said to them, "that I am going in there to get Rene out here. Then, wait in the kitchen until I actually get her into the living room. When I have her screaming 'cause I'm tickling her, you guys come running to her rescue and beat the snot out of me."

"YEAH!" James jumped up and hustled into the kitchen.

Rachel kept her eye on me. A little protective of her sister, she knew this was risky. It could backfire.

I knocked on Rene's bedroom door.

"Yeah?"

"It's Dad."

"Yeah, come in."

I walked over to the bed where she sat doing her homework.

"Mind if I sit down?"

"Have a seat," she moved some notebooks aside to make room for me.

"They tire you out?"

"Yeah," I said. "I actually wanted to talk to you about that."

"What is it?" She set her book down and looked at me.

"Well, I was thinking about how much the little ones like to wrestle. And then I was thinking about when I was young and I'd wrestle with my own Dad."

She looked straight at me.

"I was thinking that you and I never really wrestled when you were younger."

She smiled and looked at me, suspiciously.

I leaned over close to her for a hug and maneuvered so I could quickly and easily snatch her up, toss her onto my shoulders and carry her out to the living room. She didn't move away from me.

"So, I was thinking," I paused, and she gave a bigger smile. "I was thinking about kicking your butt."

My swift movements even surprised me. I hoisted her up onto my shoulders and carried her down the hallway toward the living room. She laughed and screamed and demanded I put her down, beating her hands almost convincingly against my back. One, two, three . . . I lifted her up off my shoulders and rolled her over to the living room floor. I tickled her, and she went ballistic. The screeching sound that came from her was loud enough to alert the National Guard.

"MOM!" she screamed.

WHAM! Rachel and James flew across the floor and slammed against me simultaneously. Their strategic attack demanded my attention. Rene got loose and spun away. As I worried about the two little ones, Rene found my feet. Her tickling caught me by surprise. She sat on my legs, and I hated that. Besides, Rachel and James occupied my upper body and, no matter how I wiggled, I couldn't shake Rene. The three of them made a formidable foe.

I knocked Rene off balance, and she bounced right back onto me. I escaped her again, and she grabbed at my legs again with determined force.

James reached into my armpit, tickling me, and Rachel attacked down at my feet with Rene. They were like forty-pound ants; fingers everywhere tickling me.

"Sara," I yelled into the kitchen, "Get them off me."

"HELP!"

"This is no fair."

"Rene! You're too big for this."

"Tough," she responded. "You're just gonna have to deal with it."

No way she was easing up.

The three of them kept at it. At the mercy of their laughter, I thought I would pee my pants. I laughed and yelled, joyfully thankful that Rene played in the fun.

"SARA!?" I pleaded.

"Oh? Now you want to stop?" She said mockingly. "Give it to him, Rene."

At some point, Rene perched herself on my torso, and Sara sat on my legs. The two little ones ran around the edges of me reaching in to land their tickles wherever I was vulnerable.

"How do you like it now, Dad?" Rene yelled triumphantly.

"I like it just fine."

The wrestling went on until they were too tired to continue holding me back. When their grips weakened, they bounced off and scattered to the edges of the room and into the kitchen looking for water.

I lay there on the floor, breathing and sweating and warily looking through my squinty eyes waiting for Round Three.

A Cup of Coffee

I drove over to the Barnes & Noble in Huntington Beach to pick up *The Sparrow*. Close to the house, I had a few hours to kill before Sara went to work—then I'd go over and be with the kids. I had moved out of the house over two months ago.

A trusted friend suggested this book, especially for what I was going through. But, what was I going through, exactly?

It would be stupid to drive thirty minutes to the apartment I stayed in for just two hours, and then drive back. I'd come from the office, barely putting in a few hours this Saturday, not wanting to be working.

I first thought I'd purchase the book and drive to the beach. Maybe sit in the sun and start reading. Pretend I was on vacation. Pretend that sitting in the sun would make a difference.

Despite the crowded mall parking lot, I found a spot near the front door. Cars, couples hand in hand, Moms with kids—the Saturday crowd scurried everywhere. The buildings at the new Bella Terra Plaza were yet unfinished. The Cheesecake Factory next door to Barnes & Noble took shape. Full signage, patio tile mapped out. A laborer in white overalls trimmed off the plastic from the windows. Yellow caution tape tied to traffic pylons protected the street and sidewalk in front of the bookstore with only a brief reprieve so customers could get in and out.

Just before entering the bookstore, the serenity kicked in—a strong, coffee-like buzz percolated. My heart sped up.

I went directly to the escalator, walked onto a step and stopped, allowing the rolling staircase to carry me up to the Information Desk on the second floor. I was second-in-line. The man with the employee-card lanyard around his neck walked the first-in-line over to her book choice, and disappeared. Waiting at the counter, the line behind me grew to include six others. One of the customers-to-be, a young man with curly, long hair and a proper English accent, recounted the historical sequence of linguistic development to his girlfriend whose arms draped around his neck. He paused his explanation only to kiss her, sensuously. Their wet lips parted, and he began again explaining where he had stopped—somewhere in sixteenth century Italy.

The young employee with her lanyard who looked up my book selection (I'd forgotten the author's name) walked me over to Science Fiction, paused, then placed her forefinger over the top of the spine of *The Sparrow* by Mary Doria Russell.

"Is this it?" she asked.

I looked at it. Science Fiction? Huh. I thought it would be under Self-Help or Spiritual Guidance or Mental Health. What was I going through? I really didn't know what kind of book I was looking for.

"Yeah, I guess that's it. Thanks."

She walked away, and I stood there flipping the pages. I read the back cover overview and a few comments by the critics—none I recognized.

Down the escalator, I looked to my right into Starbucks. No line at the counter.

I paid for the book and walked directly into Starbucks. I scratched the sitting-in-the-sun idea and opted instead for a cup of coffee and a few hours among strangers, reading quietly. Grande mild, room for cream.

An upholstered chair was empty. I eased myself into it, half-expecting the party to my left or right to claim their friend would be right back. But the woman next to me nodded her approval. She discussed with her friend the merits of The Da Vinci Code movie that had opened just last week. They talked about The Louvre and The Pyramid.

The one woman had visited, "It was huge, cavernous."

The other woman went to see the movie with a Frenchman, "They really do drive like that there," he had told her.

Another woman, further over, turned to say, "It's just a novel. What's the fuss about? No one expects it to be true."

I read the first two pages of *The Sparrow* twice. The author introduced new characters, and I couldn't keep straight which Jesuit priest was who.

The women next to me interjected Tom Hanks' character's name into my confusion.

On the other side of me, my Columbia Blue upholstered chair had a twin. Between the two twins, a round, wooden-top Starbucks table sat just below the arms of both chairs. In the center of the crowded tabletop, a sports page almost covered the edges of the crusts of two pizza slices, pepperoni. But, they weren't eaten all the way to the crust. About an inch and a half of good pizza remained on each slice. A crumpled Starbucks napkin and a Starbucks clear, plastic water cup were over next to the window. A white, venti coffee cup stood as the tall tower in the landscape.

I set my Grande cup closer to my chair, pushing aside the clutter so I'd have enough room. I now noticed the other coffee cup didn't have its brown, cardboard sleeve. Just coffee stains dripped down its whiteness toward the green Starbucks logo.

Then, I glanced at the woman sitting next to me in the other Columbia Blue chair. She wore black, oversized sunglasses. She appeared preoccupied and had long, deep lines on her face. She wore a thick knitted, long-sleeve sweater with no visible sign of breasts. Lengths of a white shirt she wore underneath her sweater snuck out of her sleeves and, at her waist, out over her lap. She moved her hands over the table as if it were hers, sliding her fingertips just above the newspaper. Her hands were those of someone who'd smoked for many years. I couldn't discern if she was forty or sixty.

I drank my coffee.

The first few sips hit my mouth bitter. I knew the taste like an old friend, and I wanted a visit. I had stopped drinking coffee after so many years of 3-4 cups a day. Actually, I had stopped many times. I read *Eat Right for Your Blood Type* and learned that coffee was detrimental to my system. Apparently, the acid in coffee teamed with my already type-O acidic stomach lining to overload me and drive me straight to irritation. Friends and family just thought I was irritated most of the time. I blame the coffee.

Supplemental to my system, Peppermint Tea provided a peaceful, alkaline calmness. I'd been drinking tea each day at work, though I'm not sure it made any difference.

Today, I wanted my coffee. I wanted to be in that bookstore. And I wanted to sit there and drink and read. I wanted to get away.

Every time I looked into the pages of my book for a world to walk into, I wandered back into the frustrations, the sadness, and the loneliness of the world I was living in. I had chosen to leave my marriage. Two months ago, after many years of thinking about it, I moved out, and I moved away from my wife and from my children. And though I tried to be available and present to my kids and what they were living through, I missed the five minutes in between everything else—the five minutes here and there that make up life everyday.

I missed the closing of the door at the end of the hall, and the clinking of the dishes brought back to the sink after dinner, and the laughter in front of the television set. I missed bumping into each other and the ensuing tickling or wrestling wars.

I sat in that blue chair wondering if I could go back. Why couldn't I go back? Why couldn't my heart think about it? I had always felt that leaving was not an option. Why was I so certain I needed to go? Why did I need to be away from Sara? If I was feeling so raw, Sara and our kids were struggling in ways I couldn't imagine. Why couldn't I go back?

And then I thought about Sara—she seemed to be far, far away. We hadn't talked for a long time. We mostly arranged things for the kids. Did I miss her? Then, I thought that maybe I missed what I hoped we had. I felt frozen, sitting there.

A Starbucks employee walked into the room with a large silver tray and offered each customer a sample bite of Chocolate Cream Crunch Cake. I took one, and the woman in the other blue chair took two.

The Da Vinci women left the store.

I dove into the second chapter of *The Sparrow*. Emilio Sandoz, a stoic Jesuit priest, had returned from interplanetary travel to Rakhat, and the other characters wanted to hear what occurred on that alien planet. They wanted to know why the other crew members failed to return with him.

And now I wanted to know. Why wasn't Sandoz telling his story, and why did my friend want me to read this book? And why was I feeling like such an alien most of the time? I felt like an alien around Sara. When I tried to explain myself, I was talking too much. When I asked for Sara to explain things, she didn't see the need to. Why was I asking her for clarification? Things were fine. Weren't they?

Out of the corner of my eye from the direction of the other blue chair, the lady with the sweater shuffled in her seat. I focused on my reading. Then, she got up and left. I finished my page as she reached the door. She slowly opened the door and strode out into the bright sunlight. The maze of caution tape across the walkway stopped her. She looked left and right.

Her right hand jutted out from her torso, and in it she carried a Starbucks cup with a brown sleeve. I immediately looked to the round table next to me and saw the other, sleeveless cup over near the window. I picked her cup up. It was empty. And my coffee cup was not on the table.

That bitch took my cup of coffee!

I stood up.

She held my cup (with the sleeve) in her right hand and a large, black carrying bag draped over her left shoulder. She waited for the cars to pass so she could cross over into the parking lot.

I searched around the room for someone to nod their head in recognition. But the two Japanese girls studied Mathematics, solving textbook equations (one sat with her feet up underneath her as she leaned across toward her friend), and the guy next to them focused on his writing on his Apple. The older gentleman there at a middle table gazed out the window in the opposite direction, deep in thought—the long, sunny, Saturday afternoon shining peacefully on his face.

That bitch took my coffee! Doesn't anybody care?

I wanted to yell out and break through the casual afternoon—let everyone know about the injustice of the crime. I wanted that coffee! Why didn't she just ask? I would've bought her a cup of her own.

She stood there just outside the glass door, waiting to cross the street.

I got up and walked to the door.

Hey, I wanted to tell her, *that's my coffee!*

I pushed the door almost open. She turned left and strolled along the storefront away from me. I half-expected her to turn back toward me to check whether she'd gotten away with it. But she didn't look back. Her shoulders were casual, normal, unworried. She'd done this before. Find a guy lost in his reading and shuffle around so he won't notice, and just get up casual as hell and walk out.

Damn.

I'd have bought her a damn coffee if she'd asked. It's just a buck-seventy. Hell, I'd have bought her a whole, damn cappuccino.

But maybe the asking was harder than the stealing. With my hand on the door, I looked at her and really saw her for the first time. She was square, frumpy, layered. Her black bag glistened in the sunlight. It wasn't a shoulder bag after all. It was a plastic trash bag.

Well, that hadn't occurred to me yet. She was homeless—or something. She needed my coffee, I told myself. The table between our chairs had her stuff on it. Time to move on, and she chose my coffee.

I returned to my chair and to my book.

The homeless woman's chair was newly occupied. That was quick. My desire to get another cup of coffee was preempted by my need to sit comfortably. I wanted a home and a chair of my own to sit in. Besides, I was already completely irritated that my cup of coffee had been stolen. With all that irritation, I didn't need more coffee. I sat and cocooned myself into the book, learning more about Emilio Sandoz, the Jesuit priest in *The Sparrow.*

A few chapters later, their perfumes caught my attention before I realized they were there. Hers delicate and sweet and too aggressive for a woman her age, and his a direct match for the first thing I heard her say, "It said on there that you were into relationships."

"Yeah," he said. "They've always been very important to me."

"How long were you married?" she asked, her hint of sarcasm beyond his grasp. I liked her unflinching interview style—direct and almost adversarial. She knew what she wanted. She wasn't looking to him for something to respond to.

I looked over toward them, where the Da Vinci women had sat earlier. Obviously their first face-to-face meeting from eHarmony or Match.com, he sat posture perfect and well dressed, Saturday casual. His shirt was pressed, a crease down the short sleeves, and he wore Dockers and colored socks. Who creases their short sleeves?

"Fourteen years," he said. "And it's been four years since the divorce."

He was probably 55 years old. I did my own math. I'm forty years old, I thought.

She didn't respond to him. I could see her hand on her coffee out of the corner of my eye without turning to look. The pause was long, and he went on, not noticing.

"We tried hard to reconcile, and even got remarried for two years before we made it final."

She listened.

"She just became angrier and angrier as time went on," he continued.

"Well, yeah," she finally weighed in. "You were good to her the first time, and she expected that again."

They went on, and on. Though they talked about books they've read, movies they've seen, and their current church of choice, she gave him very little. They shared about their children, their work, and their friends. But, they sounded like strangers being strangers, each on either side of the conversation—neither willing to build a bridge.

"I don't care if men my age," she eventually offered, "want younger women. If they want younger women, there's a reason for that and they don't want me. I'm not interested in men who aren't interested in me for who I am—and currently I'm just older."

I craned my neck over to look, and she was right. She easily looked ten years older than he did, maybe fifteen. But, she was clearly more attractive and easier to listen to. He sounded canned, almost rehearsed, trying to impress her. She was free to say anything that came to her mind, and she did. I didn't think they made a match.

But, what made a match? A long time ago, I thought I knew. I thought that building bridges made a match. The actions toward one another made a match work. I felt the more I tried to build a bridge in my marriage—the more I was repelled and sent away. Then, I thought of the many mistakes I'd made, and the ways I'd hurt Sara. And the so many ways I'd lied to myself. I was tired of shutting myself down. I didn't want to become another expendable man. But then, here I sat alone.

I looked out the window into the sunny afternoon. Then, I got up and walked out the door, looking forward to seeing my kids.

Snails are Nocturnal

With the afternoon sunshine behind me, I turned my key in the white front door, pushed and walked into the living room.

"Hi, Dad." Without looking, Patrick knew it was me. He immediately explained the details of the new game he played on his new Wii Game System. His body twisted and turned to something on the TV screen. His arm swooped and swung the controller.

"See." He swung it again. "You can turn it like this, and it follows you."

With 5pm baseball practice at a field down the street and across the boulevard, eleven year old Patrick waited after school for me to pick him up and take him. The first one home from school, he played his new Wii in the darkness. The living room blinds shut out the afternoon sunshine, closed from the night before.

The cereal bowl with his spoon in the milk sat next to an inside-out Snickers wrapper on the coffee table. A load of clean laundry draped over the large recliner. His baseball gear, bat and helmet and cleats, waited next to the chair. They had been waiting there since his practice two nights before.

I walked into the kitchen and poured myself a glass of water, then put it down empty on the counter next to the sink. Dishes filled the sink, some smeared with what looked like streaks of sour cream. Rice lingered around the sides of a large pot, and separated bowls spread across the counter. The dirty dinner plates smashed brown potato peels at the bottom of the white sink. I thought about cleaning the kitchen, but the clock above the window said we only had about five minutes before we had to leave to be on time. Besides, I hate doing the dishes.

Patrick focused on his game in the living room. His eyes wide, the white Wii controller stemmed out from the end of his hand. The strap flapped around his wrist.

"Ready to go?"

"Yeah." He didn't turn around. "Just a minute."

He didn't look to me like he intended to leave any time soon. I sat on the couch and waited. Rest a few minutes. Let him play his game. He knew the time, and his coach had instilled the importance of being early to practice. I chose to allow him to burn up a little more time.

I thought I might grab the other controller and try to learn the game with him. I wanted to. I wanted him to have me beside him playing the game. But I didn't want to move. I was tired from the day.

"We need to get going, Patrick."

"Oh, you're right," he said, and he paused the game, then shut it down, then turned off the TV and bounced up down the hallway to his room. The door closed. Two minutes later the door opened, and he strolled toward me wearing his red socks, his dirty white practice baseball pants and his red sleeves.

"Come on," he bent down and picked up his gear.

I guessed he would put his cleats on in the car. I followed him out the front door. When we got into my truck and drove off toward his practice, he immediately slipped on his cleats and tied up the strings. He then looked out the passenger window. His seatbelt was buckled. I reached over my chest and pulled my own seatbelt across to the click.

Since his Mom and I broke up, I worried that Patrick had a heavy heart and that he hung onto a sad and lonely anger that kept him adrift in his thoughts. I drove on, both hands on the wheel, searching forward. The silence between us lay like a predawn blanket of clouds on a foggy, wet hillside. I hoped if I spoke a little, he'd begin to share what he was thinking about.

"You alright?"

"Yep."

He gazed out of his window. I looked again, paused, and hoped he'd turn toward me. But he lingered there, thinking, mulling it over, I guessed, adjusting the pearl again and again in his mind. Or maybe I had no idea what was on his mind.

"What are you thinking about?" Maybe I shouldn't pry, I thought. Maybe I should just wait until he wants to say something. Maybe he doesn't want to talk about it right now. Maybe he doesn't want to talk to me.

Sitting in my truck with Patrick and driving to baseball practice, I noticed my confidence as a father had evaporated. The doubts were planted everywhere in my thinking, and I went step by step through the minefield each moment I tried to interact with either of my children. Since I had moved out of the house, I looked for opportunities to check in with them and see how they were doing.

I wanted to talk with them, and yet I didn't want to impose my concerns into the conversation. I created the separation, so why should they have to communicate on my terms, when I was ready, when I was available? I wanted to know how they were but, mostly, I wasn't around. When we were together, we went to and from school and games and practices and eating meals in a hurry. As normal as possible but not normal at all, we did the business of the day. I didn't really know how they were feeling about the separation between their Mom and me—or about the separation between me and them. And I missed them. I missed everything about them.

Our oldest daughter was living out on her own, and she avoided me. Ignored me, really. She didn't answer my phone calls or voice mails or text messages. She only came to one or two of Patrick's baseball games, even though she lived close by. This avoidance was probably age-appropriate. I thought I somehow caused it. I missed her. I was angry at her silence. I felt that ignoring someone was the rudest of all treatments. She's pissed at me. And then I thought I probably deserved it, ignoring her mother in the rudest of all ways.

Our next oldest, Rachel, was 17 years old and a busy, high school senior. She planned a three-week trip to Europe after graduation. I wondered if keeping busy was her way of avoiding the whole thing. She seemed healthy—making her life work.

I could see how I avoided long conversations with my son, James. I didn't know what to say to him. He was fifteen, and my leaving was an affront to his sensibilities. I didn't have a satisfying explanation for him, and I could see how my lack of straightforward communication hit him as an odd betrayal by a father who always believed that communication was the very key to healthy relationships.

"Well . . ." Patrick looked right at me, like now was the time. "You know. Dad." And when he paused, I had a heightened pang of hurt and sadness and empathy for his little broken heart. What was he thinking? How was this all affecting him?

"Dad?"

"Yeah?"

"You know." He turned his whole body in the passenger seat toward me. "I was thinking that snails are nocturnal. You just never see them during the day. I mean, they don't come out. And then in the morning, all you see is the trail they leave behind."

He continued, "What do you think that stuff is that makes the trail? You think it's just their wet skin dragging along the ground that makes the trail? I wonder if they secrete anything." He blinked his eyes and looked downward like *that was a weird thought.*

Secrete? I had to remind myself to turn back and watch the road in front of me.

"I don't know," he said. "That's what I was thinking."

I kept driving, looking forward and making my way toward his practice. I thought I should respond to this. Say something. Be part of *his* conversation. Maybe ask him more questions about snails.

"What do you think, Dad?"

"I don't know, Patrick. I never thought of it before. Not like that." I wondered if this was something they studied in science class at school. Or if he'd seen a show on The Discovery Channel about snails. Was that accurate? Were they nocturnal?

"Well," he drove the conversation further. "You just never see them out during the day."

"I think the sun would burn them up."

"Yeah," he added. "You rarely see them out of their shell. I mean even if they're crawling around, they're usually tight up in there. They don't usually stretch themselves out."

People are like that, I thought. Very few people stretch themselves out into areas that don't appear to be safe—or familiar. When it feels like too much, they pull back and retreat safely into their shells.

I do that, I thought. I like to think of myself as someone who goes out on a limb and explores life. But, really, I play it safe. I have to remind myself to live life fully, to try new things, to risk myself outside of my shell. So many people have argued with me that it's stupid to be out in the sun, exposed. That's the very reason we have the fears we have, they'd say, to protect us so we don't get burned.

"What do you think, Dad?"

"You mean, what was I thinking just then?"

"Yeah."

"I was thinking that people are like that."

"Like what?"

"Like snails."

"How are people like snails?" He scrunched up his nose at me.

"We don't like to stretch ourselves out. We don't want to be exposed. We like what we know, and we have a hard time trying new things." Maybe I should have just shut up. He was just talking about snails. He wasn't even thinking about his Mom and me.

"I think . . ." he said, thinking aloud, ". . . snails only come out of their shells for survival. Like they don't really need to go anywhere. As long as they have enough food."

"Yeah," I said. "I think you're right."

By this time, we were at the field for his practice. I pulled alongside the fence to the opening he could squeeze through, and we saw his team gathering around a backstop, each player reaching into his bag for his gear.

Patrick sat with me for a minute. His gear was ready to go. He had his cleats on, all tied up. We had already discussed that his Mom would pick him up at 7PM.

He looked at me, thinking about snails, I guessed.

Then, he said, "That would be a weird way to live."

I nodded my head. "I think you're right," I said.

"Good night, Dad." He left the truck.

"Good night, Patrick."

I watched him walk to practice, carrying his gear.

Jumping Rope

My wife and I stayed in the kitchen for over an hour last night discussing our life together and the pain and the struggle and the misperceptions we've each had over the past twelve years. This was the longest time we'd spent in a room together since I can recall. I moved out last March and am living with friends thirty miles away. It was the longest conversation we've had in over a year

She was angry, and I was angry. But last night, we spoke to one another. At times we yelled, taking turns attempting to convince the other we were right about something. Last night, I saw us each trying to say something to the other, trying to be heard. And I could see us each reaching across to hear what the other was saying.

I recognized that we had spent most of our married life trying to have a relationship different than the one in front of us. I felt criticized and unsupported and unheard, and she felt criticized and betrayed and lied to. She wanted protection and security. I wanted partnership and interaction. Neither one of us were satisfied with what we got.

I said some things in a way that I think she heard me last night—explained myself a little more. And I was glad to have stayed with her and said what was on my mind. For so long now, I'd been thinking of things to say and not saying them.

During the late drive home last night, I tried to calm myself and relax. Unrelated thoughts kept floating across my mind. I pushed them out, hoping to focus on the conversation we just had. But business decisions wandered in, then something my son said earlier, and the schedule for the weekend, and I'm glad to be off work tomorrow, and then I wondered what's happening for Easter. Are we going to eat together? Maybe she doesn't want me there, and should I try to make it happen . . .

Then, I remembered in the eighth grade, our assistant basketball coach was kind enough to find something I was good at. Each day, we began with a pre-assigned number of jump ropes to complete before we could participate in practice. Even those who showed up late did their jumps before getting on the court.

This worked in my favor, because our starting lineup was all veterans—limber, able-bodied boys who'd spent hours shooting and mastering the art of the dribble. They were the kings of the playground. Bryon shot from the baseline (either side), Mike commanded the range from above the key, and Chris dribbled full speed ahead and never had to look where he passed. Victor and the others, too, each had their thing. And together they were unstoppable.

I was an awkward and lanky collection of legs and arms, and adding a basketball to my running was like throwing a stick into the spokes of a bicycle—fundamentally unsound.

But I was aggressive, and I could jump rope.

For three years prior, I had played on a local Pop Warner football team, and my coach was an ex-Stanford lineman who was also a best-selling author. He knew the mechanics of growing an athlete. He taught me to jump rope, and he tested me often in the one-minute and three-minute jumping sprints. It took me a while, but once I got proficient at the sprints, Coach Allen taught me to cross over and to double and triple jump. He encouraged me and counted my jumps and kept score for me. I got good enough to feel like it was mine.

So, when I tried out for basketball my eighth grade year, I hardly expected to make the team. I played basketball with these guys at recess, and they were so much better and fluid than I was. They spoke in a silent language on the court—nodding their heads at one another toward a phantom pass or waving one another down the court toward something I couldn't see. They played with a mutual understanding and a swaggering bravado.

I, on the other hand, played basketball with a rising anxiety that anticipated my first air ball, or throwing the ball out of bounds toward a disappearing teammate, or falling over my own feet. I lived with fear and embarrassment and perpetual scabs on my elbows from sliding along the asphalt court that doubled as the church parking lot.

The first day of tryouts that year, Assistant Coach Lynch introduced us to the jump rope. He said it was an essential tool to coordinate our young bodies, to help us jump higher, and to give us an edge athletically over the competition. He did a short demonstration. Then, one by one he had us step up and give it a trial jump. The kings of the playground jumped, but this was not their thing. This was not something they had done before. They didn't have Coach Allen cheering them on. They each were awkward, tripping over the rope, and Mike fell forward before he caught himself. Some of the boys hop-skipped like the girls do.

When it was my turn and Coach Lynch called my name, I stepped up and thought this was completely unfair. Here we were at basketball tryouts, and the first thing Lynch was having us do was the thing I was best at. And I knew I wasn't any good at things that win basketball games. I thought maybe I should tell him, give him the disclaimer so he didn't expect me also to shoot from the outside or dribble the distance without looking down at the ball.

I didn't tell him, and the kings already knew I couldn't play ball. But the kings didn't know I could jump.

I took a good, deep breath and began with a slow rhythm. I picked up speed and then continued at a strong pace. My jumping was like dancing, and I did about 75-85 jumps in a row before I stopped.

I looked to Coach Lynch. He smiled.

"Can you do anything else?" He asked.

I nodded.

"Go ahead."

I looked at the other boys and saw they were also interested.

I gathered myself and began jumping at top speed. I moved rhythmically, and weaved left then right. Then, I danced on one foot and then the other. These were all things I had practiced with Coach Allen. At the time, I thought it was just for football. But now I was certainly getting the attention of the basketball coach.

"Have you ever crossed over?" He asked when I stopped for a breath.

I nodded again.

He smiled and said, "Let's see it."

I was a little reluctant to keep going. But something in me knew this was my tryout. This was my whole game. If I was going to have any chance of making this team, I'd better do my best when the coach asked for it.

This time, I jumped more deliberately, gauging my move into the crossover as if I were jumping onto a moving train. I was nervous to screw it up.

The crossover delivered, and I kept switching my hands back and forth, crossing over and over and over again.

"Good," Coach Lynch said, jotting a note down on his clipboard. "We'll be able to use you."

That was it.

The pressure was off.

I participated in tryouts for the rest of the day. I fumbled my dribbling, shanked my shots, and banged heartily into the other players for rebounds. But nothing else mattered to Coach Lynch. I was the guy who could jump rope. I had dutifully impressed him enough that he wanted me on the team.

And during the season, I became the sixth man. Essentially, I was put into the game to neutralize our opponents' best players. Because I couldn't shoot or handle the ball, I learned to play defense, and I played aggressively. It was a little different than playing linebacker, but the concept of keeping your man out of the box was similar to fighting off a blocking guard in football. And Coach used my fouls judiciously. Just as I was getting over being jittery from being in the game, he would pull me out and put in one of the top five.

When I came over to the bench, he congratulated me—though I didn't know what for. I hadn't made any baskets. I hadn't even touched the ball.

It dawned on me while I was driving home last night that Coach Lynch didn't need me to make baskets. But up to that point, baskets were all I could understand would make a difference in the game of basketball. I didn't think defense had much to do with the sport. And I certainly had no clue about managing fouls. Prior to Coach Lynch, I thought fouls were a bad thing. He taught me that there was an acceptable level of play where fouls occurred. They even measured into the strategy of the game.

I got off the freeway and turned left up to where I was staying, thinking about basketball and jumping rope, and what the hell did they have to do with the conversation Sara and I had tonight? Thinking maybe my thinking was too jumbled up with sports. Wondering who I would have been as a man if I hadn't played so many sports. Maybe I'd be someone who knew other things—knew what love was.

I kept thinking about why I left and what I wanted. And then it struck me that I had been trying to make baskets in my marriage. Score the way I know how. And I couldn't see how she was trying to score, how she wanted her life to be. And I wanted to say things that were on my mind and be heard, but somewhere along the line I learned not to push.

I parked the car and sat there for a moment. For many years now, instead of saying what was on my mind, I just tried to avoid causing fouls.

Football La Femme

Last night's powder puff football game was scheduled to kick off at 7pm.

Our girls arrived on campus at 4pm for the pre-game meal up in the Blue Room. We had lasagna and spaghetti, water and Gatorade. We talked about keeping our energy under the lid until game time, but the girls chattered incessantly and their noise filled the echoing room.

They dolled up their black under-eyes with blue eye shadow and blue lipstick, and the hair train snaked across the tile floor. They wrapped blue bandanas around their braided hair. Their black, tight pants were accented with knee-high, white and royal fat-striped socks, and their royal jerseys said Duckaneers across the front in athletic gold. Some wore black Under Armor shirts beneath their jerseys.

We counted players and arranged positions and melted plastic mouthpieces to fit.

Sometime before 5pm, while counting the players, I noticed our starting QB wasn't there yet. Her Mom was serving the other girls dinner, but Michelle wasn't there. And Jen, one of our more dominating offensive linemen, wasn't there. And my daughter, Rachel, and her friend Julia weren't there yet. And their friend Jennifer wasn't there, either.

Me and a couple girls flipped open our cell phones, and we called looking for the missing players.

"Rachel, where are you?"

"We're in the parking lot, Dad. Coming up."

"Where were you? It's quarter to five?"

"Dad, we went to Target to get some stuff. Wait until you see our shorts. I'll be right there. I've got Aubrey and Julia and Jennifer with me. I'm so excited. I can't wait until game time. You'll love our shorts."

Within minutes, the missing girls arrived. More lasagna served. More hair braiding. More blue make-up. And the hallway outside the Blue Room filled with outfitted girls going down to the bathroom and back.

Our kickers and QBs and receivers went onto the field for early warm-ups, and they were greeted by a green Kerminators jersey worn by a coach for the senior team. He taunted our players, "Get ready to get your butts kicked, Juniors."

Coach Mike remained quiet, knowing the danger of early assessments. Our girls knew to listen hard, take the field intent, and prepare for game time. They knew the make-up and the chatter and the pre-game noise from either team meant nothing. We repeated this at every practice: composure, preparation and playing hard will win the game—and winning the game will be fun.

The rest of our team took the field for warm ups. We ran, threw and blocked. We lined up, did our jumping jacks (the whole back row was out of sync and off count and did half a jump more than the rest of the team), and then we gathered over by the forty-yard line for our team photos.

Then, during our pre-game scrimmage, one of our team Moms overheard another green Kerminator coach evaluating and mocking our talent to his team. Too slow. Can't block. No speed. Play's too simple. Look awkward. They're not even athletes. What's with all the blue make-up? Those running backs are stocky. Can't throw. Look, she dropped the ball.

During the scrimmage, Rachel (our middle linebacker and kicker) let me know she wasn't going to do the kickoff.

"Why not?" I asked.

"Dad. I can't. I'm not any good at it."

She ran past me to the defensive huddle and shouted over her shoulder, "Don't worry. Luna's gonna do it."

Yeah, I thought, but we didn't practice with Luna doing it.

They broke the huddle and defended the play. Rachel saw me looking at her and stopped. She put her hands out, asking what I wanted.

"Are you wearing *boxer* shorts?" Her shorts were bright yellow flannel with some sort of red characters on them. The yellow shorts were outside her normal, black-legged tights. The fly stayed shut, but these were obviously men's underwear.

"Yeah! Julia and Jennifer have the same ones!" She beamed and bopped back to the huddle.

After a few moments, Luna ran by, returning from her last offensive play.

"You're kicking?" I asked.

"Yeah!" She smiled.

"Mike?" I found Coach Mike. "Luna's kicking?"

"Yeah, it'll be fine. She did a few off the tee, and she was great. Rachel shanked everyone she tried out there. She'll still do the punting, though."

I was glad he had that handled.

I turned to watch the next scrimmage play. We ran a QB sweep right with our wing-T running backs leading the way. Michelle sped around the end and up the field to the end zone. I was confident she was going to have a good game. Fast, smart and competitive.

But what caught my eye was Kluver. She had a defender in a headlock, and she was whipping the girl over her leg, trying to flip her, throw her down. The defender fought out of the hold and hurried back to the defensive huddle.

"Kluver!?" I stood there with my mouth open, looking at her.

She came and stood next to me, like I was going to say something to her. She looked at me.

"I'm not supposed to do that? Huh?"

"Well, you know." I paused. I was torn. I was supposed to coach her.

Of course, she wasn't supposed to do that—wrestling moves on the football field. But this was Kluver. This was the sheepish redhead that took the entire six weeks of practices before the game, and we never found her aggressive genes. She smiled at every practice. When I showed her how to block—knock the girl back and run her over—she smiled every time and nodded her head, like she completely understood the concept. But during each practice scrimmage, she merely ran up next to the defender and followed her around. The physical contact eluded her.

The physical contact eluded many of the girls. I kept showing them how to do it, how to hit and push and drive their legs so the defender would eventually give in to their relentless, annoying presence on the field—how to make themselves (as blockers) the defenders' concern. Once the defender is thinking always of you, and where you are, and when you're going to hit them next—then our runners are free to run, flying past the defense in that split second of concern.

But at practice, they'd nod their heads like they understood, and then they'd go run a play and merely get close to the defender; rub their shoulder up near them, or lean against them, or chase them. And the defender ran free to grab our runner's flag.

At practice, our offensive line and our running backs returned to the huddle smiling.

"Why are you smiling?" I asked before calling the next play.

No answer. Big smiles.

"Girls. Listen!" Don't get too frustrated, I reminded myself. They're trying. They have no idea the aggression you're speaking about.

"Girls," I went on, "the seniors are not playing a football game. They're out to beat the crap out of you. They're going to hit, kick, scratch and claw you. They lost last year. This is all about pride for them. No way in hell they're going to lose this game. And you don't have a chance unless you get aggressive and show them you're in this for real."

All smiles.

"Look! They're going to beat the crap out of you. I'm not talking about the score. They want to hurt you."

Smiles.

"Look." I grabbed a girl and told her to get in her stance. I got down across from her and was about to show her a solid block when I stood up. *What the hell am I doing? I can't knock this girl around.* I looked across the field to where Coach Mike and Coach Mark were working with the defense.

"Mike!" I yelled. "Give me Rachel for a minute."

He waved her over, and she ran to me.

"Rachel, look. I'm trying to show them how to block, and I can't knock down someone else's daughter. So, I'm going to show them on you."

She nodded her head and set her one foot back ready for contact.

"No, I'm serious. I'm going to knock you down and run you over."

"I know, Dad. Just go ahead. We gotta do this. We're going to win this game."

So, I ran her over. We had wrestled and rumbled enough for her to be safe with this. When she got up the first time, we went again. But, this time I showed the offense how to control the defender by grabbing their shirt under the armpits and throwing them opposite from where our runner was going. Each time, Rachel popped up ready to go. She's resilient, I thought. This is why she's our middle linebacker.

"Kluver, you got any brothers at home?" I asked during one particularly frustrating practice.

She shook her head, No. Of course, I thought.

I turned my shoulder toward her and said, "Here. Just give me a punch and get it over with." But she wouldn't do it.

I told her that someone was going to play fullback for us, and that if she didn't learn to hit and block, then Tricia would play most of the game rather than her. We both knew Tricia would hit someone. I didn't know then that I hit Kluver's button.

Here she was the day of the game, trying to rip off the head of the defender—during the scrimmage, her own teammate.

"Kluver," I said. She was standing there next to me—game day—eager to hear what I had to say. "You do it however you want to do it. We'll make the Refs call it and stop you."

"Thanks, Coach." She smiled and ran back to the offensive huddle.

I looked over to the home sidelines. The green senior jerseys wandered around. Two green jerseys walked across the track and onto the field. Their sports bags were slung over their shoulders. Some of their players were just arriving. I spotted their coaches and Debi, the administrator in charge of the evening. But I didn't see what I wanted to see. Ten minutes to go and no referees.

We took our girls back up to the Blue Room to settle down, gather. Take a knee. But the girls didn't want to kneel down on the tile floor.

"Can we just stand?"

Again, their echoing cackle filled the room.

With some waving of arms, the girls quieted and readied for the field. We circled together for the final words.

"Shhh. Shhhh. Shhh," the girls chimed.

Our offensive tackle, though, sat against the back wall with her feet up on a chair and with her cell phone in her ear. Two girls approached me from out of the group, wanting to leave the room, holding hands and walking toward the door.

"Where you going? We're almost ready to take the field?"

The one girl pointed to her friend and said to me, "She's on her period."

Then, "Come on," to her friend. She grabbed her by the wrist, and they disappeared down the hall to the bathroom. I saw their names and numbers as they went, but I don't remember who it was.

I looked back into the room. The team was gathered, all eager and smiling and worried about the game. Some looked like they were going to cry.

"All right, ladies," I started. They stopped into silence and looked to me.

A girl raised her hand. I nodded and acknowledged her, thinking she wanted to offer her team words for the war.

"I don't have a mouthpiece," she said. This was a problem she thought I should solve.

Pause and breathe. Don't say anything sarcastic, Coach. She's a player on your team, and she needs a mouthpiece. I looked for and caught the eyes of Ashley's Mom. She had been the go-to person for all the questions I had during the weeks of preparation for the game. At practices, she made sure we took roll, and she easily handled the team meal and organized whatever we needed. Silently, I pleaded with my eyes for her to take this girl and satisfy her dilemma. And she did. The girl understood and walked over to Mrs. Flores.

Then again, behind the last girl of the group, I saw our offensive tackle still on the phone, still seated in her chair by the back wall—her feet still up and her eyes dazing off into her conversation.

I stopped. I looked only at her. The room turned all eyes toward her.

"Jen! Jen! Jen!" They all laughed and called her name, but she saw nothing and continued to talk into her phone, eyes off in some other world.

"JEN!" I got her attention. She looked at me questioningly—like, why was I bothering her?

"Jen. Off the phone."

She moved the phone slightly away from her mouth and softly let me know it was her Mom she was talking to.

"Off the phone."

"It's my Mom," she insisted.

"Off the phone. Now."

Her eyes widened.

"NOW!"

"Mom," she spoke deliberately, "I need to get off the phone." Both her and her Mom understood that my request was ridiculous. "I can't talk right now, Mom. I gotta go play the game."

Then, Jen looked at me and gave me all her attention.

"Are you ready?" I asked her.

She nodded her head.

"Are you ready for *football?*"

She nodded. Her eyes widened, and she was with me now.

"Good. Because the game starts now."

I said whatever I said to the team. I wanted them to know they were ready and that they had done a great job practicing and preparing for the game. Six weeks of practices and meetings and getting their bodies and minds wrapped around what it meant to be football players, to put all the pieces together to be a football team. I let them know they were a talented group of athletes and that I was proud of them for their eagerness and willingness and their courage to learn a new game, to learn to be both aggressive and smart.

When I was done, I looked around, found and nodded to Coach Joe. We needed to do something else, the cheering and excitement part, and he was our guy. I stepped back from the circle of girls, and Joe stepped in. They surrounded him. All hands went up, and he yelled a few lines and the girls responded, hands waving and high-fiving, and now they began bouncing up and down on their toes.

I didn't hear it, but the vibration of my cell phone in my front pants pocket alerted me. I flipped it open, said hello, and the woman on the other end said the referees had arrived and were ready to meet with the coaches.

It took me a few attempts to extract Joe from the circle of girls. He couldn't hear me. When he finally heard me yell, We Gotta Go, he turned to the team and said, "Okay, girls, it's game time. Let's go out there and kick their butts!"

I was standing in the doorway when the team broke and the sea of blue stormed in my direction. I put my hands up to stop them.

"Joe. Just you. The referees want to meet with the coaches first."

"Oh. Yeah." He smiled and his face was game-ready, but his eyes were tired from a long day at work, and he had driven to our game from the Varsity and JV softball (Away) games he coached earlier that afternoon. He and the five Duckaneers who were also on his softball team hurried over for a quick bite of lasagna before throwing on their jerseys for our team photo. Joe still had the orange long sleeves of his softball windshirt sticking out from under his new royal game jersey.

Joe and Mike and I walked from the Blue Room to the field. We were quiet.

My phone rang from my pocket again. The Rocky theme played until I flipped it open.

The woman on the other end asked me whether I knew of any students who could hold the sticks. We needed three.

I walked on in silence for two or three long steps. We don't have anyone to hold the sticks. And she's calling me now as I'm walking on the field to figure this out.

"Let me see what I can do," I told her.

I sent Joe and Mike over to where the referees and the coaches from the other team, the green senior Kerminators, were waiting, and I walked up to the first row of seats in the stadium, looking to recognize any student of mine. I saw Bobby Chacon. He was seated amongst six other students, his backpack on his back.

He saw me coming.

"Bobby, would you do the down markers?" He came down over to the railing.

"What?"

"Would you do the down markers? We need three of you," I pointed to the guys sitting up behind him. "You'd be on the field. On the visitor side. With the juniors."

Bobby was a sophomore, and I figured I'd have better luck if he knew he'd be the only male student over on the other sideline with the girls.

"I can't." He didn't want to say No to me. "I can't. My Mom's on her way, and I'm leaving."

"Yeah, don't worry about it. I'll see you tomorrow."

Good enough, I thought. I tried.

Then, I looked up into the stands and saw the crowd filling in. The lights in the press box were on. Three parents were standing behind their tripods. The girls' principal was sitting at the announcer's microphone, and I recognized Jeff, our Assistant Activities Director, sitting next to her.

This is going to be fun, I thought.

I met up with the coaches and the Refs. Then, our captains met with the Refs. We won the toss and deferred, choosing to be on defense first. I thought our defense was the strongest part of our team.

I stood on the far sideline, away from the packed grandstand, and watched our kickoff team string like pearls across the field. Our girls on the sideline were standing on their toes, in bunches, their anxious eyes skittering back and forth until as a team they looked over to Luna. Luna adjusted the ball on the tee and stepped back. She looked to the Ref, waited for the whistle, then sent the ball high up into the lights, end-over-end downfield to the twenty yard line. Our team streaked down their lanes and converged on the kick returner.

After the kickoff, it was first down, their ball, but no down markers. I looked along our sidelines and saw the Ref who was spotting the line of scrimmage—but there were no sticks behind him. I looked beyond him, all along our sidelines, but the sticks weren't even out on the field. He saw me coming and raised his eyes, like I was supposed to know something. I didn't know anything.

My job was to get fifty teenage girls ready to play a football game. They're ready. We just kicked the ball into the lights. I don't know who's doing the damn sticks.

The Ref out on the field got done talking to the coach from the other side and walked in my direction. When he got close enough, he yelled out that we'll just use the twenty, the forties and the other twenty for first downs. My mind searched for some recognition of this. But, I'd never played *flag* football before.

I looked over to Coach Joe, and he waved it on. No problem. But—we didn't practice it like that.

"It's fine, Coach. Let's go."

I waved to the Ref on the field. No problem. But, I was concerned. How was I going to get that into the girls' minds? The game was already going.

"Mike!" Coach Mike looked at me. "They got to get to the forty for a first down."

He knew this. I pointed out to the field. Our defense was huddled at the ball.

"Tell them," I yelled. "Rachel needs to know."

Then, I walked further down the sideline over to Joe. He was huddled with the offense, preparing for the first series. I put my hand on his shoulder.

"Make sure they understand the first down."

I walked away and heard him explicitly telling the girls the deal with the first downs.

We held their offense. They punted.

Our offense took the field, and immediately lined up at the line of scrimmage. No huddle. This was the play Joe was excited about—line up nine players away from the ball over near the sideline and see if they adjust, or call timeout. They did neither. Nothing. They're in trouble, I thought.

Michelle, our QB, called the huddle for the next play and showed the girls the diagram on the white notecard she'd received from Coach Joe. Then, on the third play, Alexis took the ball, swept around the corner, and raced to the sideline then up the field for the first score of the game. Just like we practiced.

Alexis made running look easy. She ran with an intensity mixed with joy. She ran with a smile on her face, leaning forward just enough to get there a step ahead of the defense. Her big eyes and graceful glide were fun to watch. She was indicative of this whole group of girls: eager, talented, fun and willing to learn. At practice, we told her to take advantage of the full field in the stadium. No one would catch her. Just race to the sidelines when we go wide and beat them to the score. She was fun to watch.

We missed the extra point, and Luna kicked off, up into the lights.

Three plays, and punt.

Next, our offense drove play after play after play after play to the fifteen-yard line, going in. I looked to Joe, and he nodded. He signaled the play into Michelle out on the field.

The play went as planned. We faked the QB sweep right. Their defense stepped up for the run and, from her tight end alignment, Luna slipped behind them into the corner of the end zone. Michelle pulled away from the pursuing defenders, stepped up on her toes and threw a strike. Touchdown!

We missed the extra point, and Luna kicked off again, up into the lights.

Their green offense started down the field. Our girls were doing their jobs. But, they kept gaining yards—play after play. I worried about the momentum turning their way. Then, they ran a play up the middle right over the guard. *That's against the rules*, I thought. At our coaches meeting before our first practice, all coaches had been told and agreed that interior running plays were dangerous and, therefore, not allowed. They ran the next play up the middle again, but to the other side.

"Hey, Ref, that's against the rules!" I walked out almost to the hash marks. He didn't turn around.

"Ref! Ref! They can't do that!"

"What?"

"They can't do that! Ask Debi over there!" I pointed to their sidelines. She was in charge of the whole game. She knew the rules.

Their tan coach with his glowing smile and straw hat was walking out onto the field. He was shrugging his shoulders.

"Come on," he said. "Let the girls play. It's just a game."

"No way!" We were at the Ref now, and the Ref was waving us both off the field, wanting to continue and get the clock running.

"We'll deal with it at the quarter," he repeated.

"No way!" I looked to the clock. "There's four minutes left. He can't just run it up the middle. Our girls aren't ready for that. Four minutes could kill them."

This is the Seniors' game, I thought. They didn't even tell the Refs the rules.

"Come on. What's the big deal?"

"He's cheating, Ref."

I walked off the field.

I walked over through our bunch of girls to Miss Palwitz. She was standing there in the freezing night breathing frost out of her down parka—the hood tied around her face. She smiled, her red cheeks popping out of her face. As our faculty advisor in charge of our team, I could see she was enjoying beating the Seniors.

One of my commitments was that she have a good time with this. I wanted her to see the girls learning and extending themselves—working hard and having fun. Her smile was a good thing for me to see.

"Do you have a phone?"

She nodded.

"Get on the phone and call Debi. Tell her that her coach is cheating over there. He's running up the middle, and that's against the rules. They can't run between the tackles. It's *Flag*. If they wanted to do that, they should've told us and we'd knock the crap out of them. It's not our fault if they don't discuss the rules before the game starts."

She nodded and called.

The rest of the first quarter and most of the second went about the same way. Their offense generated some yards. Our offense also moved the ball. Again, though, I worried they would score and our girls would get down, frustrated, maybe give them an opening. I wanted to stop any hope they had of catching up.

Stephanie was in now at QB for us. *I hope she doesn't fumble.* The first few practices she attended, she fumbled the ball from center. I tried to show her how to open her hands and place them up under the center, let the center pop it up into her hands automatically. But, she kept reaching for the ball—trying to grab it. And she kept fumbling it. We couldn't get a play off. Michelle attended club soccer practice that day, and we needed another QB. Stephanie was getting frustrated, but if she couldn't take the hike then she couldn't play QB.

I told her that her fingers were in the pathway of the ball. If the center hikes it up with any velocity (like she's supposed to) she's going to break a finger.

After explaining it to her again and getting the same dismal result, I looked at Nellie, our center, and Nellie looked at me like *What are you thinking?* I decided I couldn't show Stephanie how to do it. I looked again over to the defense and yelled for Rachel. She ran over. I told Rachel the problem. I can't really show Stephanie what I want. I'm not going to touch you, I said. I'm just going to push Stephanie's hands and fingers up to where I want them.

Rachel bent over the ball, and Stephanie stepped up to take the hike. She put her hands where she had put them before. I got down on one knee and pushed Stephanie's top hand up against Rachel's butt, and then I told her to stretch her fingers forward, explaining to Stephanie that she's not supposed to be thinking about the ball. I pushed her fingers up further. Let it pop up into her hands and be looking at the defense, thinking of how we're going to beat them on this next play. Open the bottom hand like this. Make a big basket for the ball and receive it.

Rachel popped the ball up there.

She did it again.

Then, we put Nellie in there, and she popped it up. Bingo.

"Thanks, Rachel."

"No problem, Dad." And she turned and bopped back to the defense.

So, I'm standing there on game night hoping Stephanie remembers to put her hands up on the center and open her fingers forward. Just before I got too concerned, she took the ball wide right around the end—I looked downfield and saw our receivers and blockers lining up against their defenders—and Stephanie scooted and shimmied and rolled sixty yards for another score. Our sideline erupted, finally believing that we would win this game. Their defense dragged themselves off over on their side.

It was 18-0 at half.

The second half was much the same, but we didn't score any more offensive touchdowns. Our offense looked polished, and I was proud of them. Coach Joe shuffled through his deck of plays on 3x5 index cards. He did a good job of mixing plays and getting the ball to different players. Our team was stacked with talent. In addition to Alexis, we had Allie and Kellie, two of the fastest girls on the field. Allie ran like a sports car, always shifting into the next gear. Kellie ran tall like a gazelle (elegant and graceful), but with the force of a thundering thoroughbred.

I was on the sideline telling our girls to show their best face to the Seniors. *Dumb Cows.* No mocking. No taunting. Just keep it cool. Don't get mixed up in their frustration and anger. They're going to try and provoke us. They're going to lose this game, and they're pissed.

I turned and looked over my shoulder. Our defense was on the field. The Seniors were throwing the ball, hoping for a lucky shot. Rachel jumped into the air from her middle linebacker position and intercepted a fifteen-yard pass. Then, with deft command of the field in front of her, she bolted toward the sideline and rounded toward the end zone and took it in.

24-0.

The remaining six minutes of the game were pure celebration for the Juniors. Miss Palwitz gave me a hug, and I thanked her for making that call. I apologized for being so riled up. She didn't care. She was celebrating. More than half the stands were jumping up and down in royal blue excitement. Our girls were jumping up and down and screaming. We herded them over to shake the Seniors' hands.

I hugged Mark and Paul and the other coaches. We were all smiles.

Afterward, after the celebration on the field, after hugging families and friends, and after the stands had cleared, and after we all made plans to celebrate at Frantone's Pizza where Coach Mike promised to buy if we had a shutout—three girls came into the Blue Room and grabbed their bags and were headed out the door.

"Hey," I stopped them. "Do you know where Chrissey is?"

Their heads all tilted the same way. Like I was joking. Like what was I saying?

"Chrissey? You know. Blonde? Defensive End? Big hair?"

One of them stepped forward. "Coach? I'm Chrissey," she said.

"You're Chrissey?"

She nodded. And I looked closer. I had no idea who this girl was. The Chrissey I knew had big, wavy blonde hair. At every practice, she dominated from the defensive end position. And she looked like a Nordic warrior out on the football field, hair flowing, big presence. She was simply unstoppable. We couldn't get past her in practice, and the Kerminators couldn't get past her tonight. I wanted to tell her she was awesome.

But this girl in front of me now had her hair braided tightly across her head. She was just an average, skinny girl. I couldn't even tell her hair was blonde.

"You're Chrissey?" I asked sheepishly.

She nodded.

I looked her straight in the eye: "You played an *awesome* game tonight."

A big, fat smile erupted across her face, and I was relieved I didn't screw that up.

"Thanks, Coach."

They left, and I picked up the last of the litter from the evening in the Blue Room. I walked out into the night air toward my truck in the parking lot. On my way, I passed up another two girls who were walking together.

"Great game tonight, Kristen." I passed them.

"Thanks, Coach."

I walked on. After about six more steps, Kristen whispered to her friend, "I didn't even know he knew my name."

Maybe the night air brought it to me.

"RED!" I said loudly.

She laughed. Every practice, Kristen wore the same red, hooded-pullover sweatshirt. Rather than try to learn her name, it just became easier to call her Red. I don't know when her real name stuck, but her teammates would always correct me whenever I'd call her in the huddle, and I'd yell out Red.

Tonight, her name came easily.

"Of course, I know who you are!" I said without looking behind me. I walked out to the parking lot feeling better than I'd felt in a long time.

The Craw II

He nudged the ceramic bowl full of chicken soup over to the side of the kitchen counter with his right hand. The right hand shook mildly, like nervous twitching. The uneven tiled counter was bumpy, especially the dips and grooves from the grout. He bent a little forward, concentrating. The soup sloshed to the rim, but not over. He'd done this before. Many times, I guessed.

Perhaps he thought he'd steady the bowl with his left hand once it got to the edge of the counter. Then, maybe, lift it up with both hands and carry it over to the dining table. But, his right hand couldn't do its part when it was time for the two hands to gather the bowl up and move it on over. His right hand kept shaking, interrupting the attempt.

I didn't think to grab the bowl and deliver it for him to his seat at the table. I wasn't yet thinking he needed any help. I hadn't made the whole leap—that he'd need me to help him with this little task. I was just visiting. My Mom must usually help him, I thought.

But she was sitting in the living room watching a documentary about John Wayne. Her back was to us. She had a glass of Chardonnay on the light stand next to her floral printed chair. She was relaxed. My Mom didn't drink much. In fact, hardly at all, and the wine glass next to her was still full.

"Did you know that John Wayne went to USC on a football scholarship?" She turned her head a half-turn toward us in the kitchen before looking back again to the TV.

I looked into the kitchen for signs of dinner. A wooden mixing spoon sat on the sink on a blue, ceramic spoon plate. I could smell the dinner in the oven. I was glad to see my Mom relaxing. She was completely efficient as a dinner host.

I liked their dance. I thought it odd that he'd be working this bowl of soup just before dinner, but my Mom was unconcerned.

My Dad turned toward me, "Will you move this bowl over to the table for me?"

"Sure."

He smiled generously, gracefully. When I put the bowl down at his seat, he settled into his chair, picked up his spoon and smiled.

I remembered something my friend said the other day. We were talking about our parents' aging and health, and I said that for 74 and 75 years old my parents were incredibly vibrant.

"I don't think I've met your Mom," she said. "But your Dad, he's a man who's aged but certainly not an old man."

His hand shook now with every swoop of his spoon. He somehow got the soup to his mouth, undeterred by the shaking.

Bent there in his chair, I was proud of him—that he paid so little attention to his shaking right hand.

We had golfed at the high school scramble tournament again this year. The first couple holes, he took an extra few moments to tee up his ball, pushing the tee down into the grass, then trying to balance the ball on the tee. His shaking hand kept knocking the ball off. Finally, with a hand on either side of the tee, he steadied enough for the ball to stay.

On the sixth or seventh hole, though, the teeing up took too long for him. Maybe he thought we were impatient. I looked to Leo, his longtime friend and business associate, and to Mike, my college coach and friend, and their faces were filled with appreciation. These men loved my Dad. We had all day. But he turned to me and smiled, and I set the ball on its perch for him.

Something about moving the bowl of soup and teeing up his golf ball touched me inside. Not that he was getting old and needed help. I actually think he could have still done both tasks with another moment or so of concentration. It was that he asked me to do these things. The invitations were simple and clear. On the golf course, he just smiled and reached out his hand with his tee and ball. In the kitchen, he asked me directly.

But I heard so much more, things I hadn't heard before.

"Son, you can help me."

"Son, care for me."

"Son, look at us growing here together."

Her Generosity

"What do you think about being Catholic?" I asked her as we left lunch at Wahoo's Fish Tacos and walked down the sidewalk to the parking lot.

"Theologically or in practice?"

"I don't know," I said.

My thinking wasn't that particular. I was just considering my own uncertainty and my waning alliance to the Church. I wondered if it was odd to be forty-two years old and unsettled about my church and my religion. A big part of me thought it was odd not to be unsettled. She grew up Catholic, like I had, and I wanted her perspective. The rules of faith had been crashing onto the broken realities of my own life for many years, and I was ready to discuss this with someone I trusted.

Stepping up into my truck on the passenger side, she thanked me for the opened door.

We spent an hour and a half at lunch. She had no urgent need to be back at work. I ate fish taquitos and fish tacos with lemonade. My plate also had white rice and black beans. She's Mexican, and I wondered as I ate whether my meal resembled anything authentic. I didn't think so. Her meal had a red sauce on it that made me think it was closer to the real thing, but I don't know why I thought that. Was anything authentically Mexican at Wahoo's?

I called her today because I was preparing a business proposal to a large corporation. They asked me to edit a book they were publishing, and they also wanted me to train their bilingual staff to write clearer English, to produce simple and clear reports. I thought I could do that, even though I didn't know any Spanish. She's a businesswoman with many years' experience working with large companies, and I was tired of having these opportunities evaporate due to my confusion around the billing rate.

"Let's find your daily rate," she said when I finished my meal and cleared the space for my yellow notepad.

"Yeah, let's do that."

"How much do you want to make a year? Just hypothetical. Play with it," she said, like it was just that simple. Her voice was kind, and her eyes smiled with a patience I appreciated. "With this work and this part of your income, just throw out a number—based solely on your whim. And don't include or even think about your teaching salary or anything else."

"I keep thinking about the projects and what I think they're worth."

"No, you're not," she said. "You're thinking about what you think *you're* worth."

She tilted her head, challenging me.

I nodded back. She was right.

I remembered once she'd told me of a business visit with a CEO at his home on a bluff in Laguna, overlooking the Pacific Ocean. The maid answered the front door, welcomed her in and led her through the dining room and into the vaulted, open living room. The whole back wall of the home was floor-to-ceiling windows with a panoramic view of the ocean. The maid walked her out to the patio to meet her host. I remember she said it was the largest home she'd ever been in.

As she walked through the rooms that day, she looked to her left and saw the cook through an open door preparing their lunch. She felt like she belonged in there, chopping vegetables, rather than on her way out to the veranda for her presentation. She called it *"Kitchen Help,"* the self-story she had that she was a Mexican woman and couldn't possibly be there for a business transaction worth over a million dollars.

"Look," she continued, "let's just figure out a daily rate and let that number drive your pricing. Forget what you think they're thinking—for right now. They obviously want you to do the work"

I got my cell phone out and calculated down from an annual salary we agreed upon as a starting point. I understood the math, but all the while I thought it didn't make sense. I only had these two projects and not a whole year's worth of work.

After I wrote down the daily rate, I looked up at her and said, "I was thinking more than that."

"How much?"

"I don't know. That just doesn't seem like enough for the amount of work."

"Are you thinking take-home, or gross? Pre-tax?" She said, thinking I hadn't thought about that—and I hadn't.

"You need to almost double it," she said, "to give you a cushion for taxes. You're an independent contractor, and the taxes are close to 50%."

I just wanted a number.

I put in another, higher annual salary and did the math and wrote it down. My eyes kept creeping further up my yellow pad to the content notes I'd taken earlier on the projects.

"What's the number you can live with?"

I gave her the number.

"Pre-tax?"

"Yes, to the customer."

Then, she proceeded to lead me through a series of questions that I had yet to ask the customer. She got me clear on how to speak with the customer to quantify what would constitute success in their eyes. What exactly did they want me to produce?

After our discussion, I felt I needed to further interview the client, and then I could submit my proposal and feel good about it. Our conversation helped me see myself working with this company, profitably.

Walking to my truck after lunch, I was thinking that her husband was a lucky guy. Last year, she married a friend of mine, the second marriage for each of them. I wanted to hear her thoughts about being Catholic and not being . . . perfect, I guess. Why would I even think perfect was possible, or worthwhile? I knew she and her husband discussed their spirituality with one another, and I'd been recently aware of my lack of desire to attend Mass any time soon. Residue, I thought, from leaving my wife of 17 years. The questions had been building for years but, of course, now I'd broken my end of the deal. I was no longer invited.

I pulled out of the parking lot after lunch to return her to work, and her voice reached me somewhere deep in my soul. Her heart spoke, and cracked. She shared beyond my question.

"If I've learned anything," she started, "it's that we're all broken somehow. And I think church should deal with our brokenness. It's how we come together, and it's how we're related to one another. There are many ways to be related in faith, and I think God wants to be in a relationship with us. And I think he wants us to be related to one another."

I agreed with that. Over the years, my experience with church was sadly unrelated. But maybe that was just me, I thought. Maybe I just kept a distance, and maybe the hunger in my own heart was a self-inflicted wound.

"I grew up," she continued, "with Mariachi bands playing in the church on Sunday mornings. We all went together. The whole family. And every Sunday, my Mom and my sisters and I stood at the kitchen sink and over the stove and made tamales. There was a rhythm and a flavor to all of it. It smelled like Mexican prayer candles and refried beans. And I remember these things, the good parts of my Catholic upbringing."

These were the markings of memory, I thought, sweetened over time, ripened through each new season. I remembered growing up in my own family, kneeling in church and looking across the backs of my brothers and sisters and to my Dad, wondering how he could kneel so straight for so long. My back hurt, and I slouched down and touched the kneeler with my hands. My younger brother looked at me like I was in trouble.

We didn't have tamales after mass. The only tamales I knew at that time were the red candies they sold at my Little League snack shack. We had fried chicken in our home, and my Mom made the best.

I drove on, and I told her, "My kids are getting older, and I wonder about their prayer life. I was thinking the other day, Sunday, that I wanted to stop in at the church with them and sit quietly and pray. It was Father's Day. I used to do that with my Dad sometimes when I was young. I hated it. But I knew as a boy it was important. I want my kids to know a relationship with God."

She nodded her head and smiled at me.

"I wonder sometimes," I continued, "if they're aware of how they're growing spiritually." Then, I thought of what I'd just been saying. My whole life I questioned the relationship between spirituality and kneeling in those pews. *God wants to be in a relationship with us. And I think he wants us to be related to one another.*

She turned and looked straight ahead.

"I think of those priests," she said, and I didn't expect it. We hadn't really been pointing toward that issue. "The carnage from the actions of a few. The destruction. The molestations, their actions, are one thing. Disgusting. But, what I can't even wrap my mind around today are the actions of the Church and the cover up. The complete inhumanity of it all. The disregard for the individuals whose lives they interrupted and changed forever.

"Maybe I could forgive, maybe, those priests for their sins. Maybe. But how can I even fathom," she gasped, "the continuous, ongoing cover up?"

I looked over to her, and her eyes ripened like old wounds. Her legs were crossed there in my truck, and she appeared poised for a battle she had fought many times. But, there was no malice in her voice, no rigid stature, no ready stance, no defensive or offensive position. She sat in a soft war of remembrance—a visitation. Her sadness was non-accusatory.

Driving her back to her work after lunch and listening to her, I nodded my head foolishly, like an understanding man who hoped to conceive of how this atrocity impacted her, thinking that we Catholics carry some shared burden for being related to this faith and the fallible men who lead us.

"I lived it," she said.

Lived what? I thought.

Then, I remembered something about her that I had forgotten. Something she had shared with me many years ago. Something she could never forget. The fog vanished, and I understood that I was a foreigner in her country and that I had no right to participate in the victory of her realizations. My participation was by invitation only. I was a visitor.

"I lived it," she said again.

I looked forward and drove the truck.

"I was twelve years old when my uncle molested me," she continued, "and that was one thing. That was bad enough. But then every single person in my family did nothing about it. Swept it under the rug. Acted like it never happened. Told me to forget about it."

She looked at me. I felt loved, and I didn't know why. I was struck by her composure. She had reached an acceptance of this volatile thing in her life and merely wanted to share it with me, peacefully, like a gift.

"You mean no one ever spoke to you about it? They never asked if you were okay?"

"Never," she said. "To this day. They just said I was crazy. Like, what was wrong with me. Even when I was dating my brother's friend, my brother told him, *Hey, you don't want to get involved with her. She's muy loca.* He never asked me what was affecting me."

She sat patiently. She had shared this with me before, but today her voice was rich, washed in her experience. Her words reached into my throat and squeezed out my air.

"I was the crazy one, but no one took the time to ask what was going on with this little girl. Why was she acting crazy? What was breaking her little heart?

"For years, I was waiting for someone to help me. I didn't know what to do. I really didn't know what was happening. Like I was drowning, and my family was all there watching but no one ever jumped in to help me.

"The first violation was a shock. It happened in a brief period of time. But the disappointment of not being cared for afterward . . . It alters who you think you are. You never think you deserve anything. It took me years. Even my Mom. She made me promise never to tell my Dad about it. It was his brother.

"The whole thing changes you at a cellular level. You're never the same. Ever. And the man who did this to me got hugs from my Mom and my Dad when he came over for dinner. For years."

We arrived at her work, and I parked near the entrance. The air-conditioning in my truck was on, the engine still running, and we turned to face one another.

"Thank you for saying this," I said. My body ached. I could barely breathe. I heard my voice as if someone else was speaking, and I sounded strangely sterile, almost academic. "I hadn't thought about the molestations in this context."

"What do you mean?"

"Well," I continued, "you've given me a broader understanding of it all. I mean, I know how a teacher impacts a classroom, and how a parent impacts a household, or how a coach impacts a team. The actions of the individuals often live within the context of the leadership provided. *Attitude reflects leadership, Captain.* And today, you've shown me the vast impact of this avoidance from the leaders in our Church.

"I used to think of the molestations as isolated cases—rogue priests affecting their victims one at a time. I see now that within the context of that leadership, how many families responded as yours did? It starts at the top. And I can only wonder at the number of young people injured by that."

I thought about her experience, her family and their avoidance of something so loud in her life. Their silence would drive me insane. I thought about the Catholic Church as I knew it. My experience. I love the individuals I know, and I've had extraordinary relationships with priests and teachers and ministers.

But, I've also known the sad and violent silence wrought from those in ministry when they are individually threatened by a system they are bound to. Are they bound to God and love and honesty and spiritual concerns, I thought, or are they bound to a system?

As the President of the Parent Board at my children's Catholic elementary school, I was personally and legally threatened by Church personnel when I asked questions about our school's finances. I was called a racist and a man who hates women by our parish Finance Manager—an Equadorian woman. I was threatened with public humiliation and legal actions if I continued my inquiry. Yet, I represented our school's parents, and our parents were concerned about our difficult financial status. They wanted answers from me.

The written lies against me were submitted to my Pastor without my initial knowledge. I continued to seek for financial clarification from our Principal, because we had work to accomplish that wasn't moving forward. But, I was met with silence from both the Principal and, then later, the Pastor. No explanation. No assistance. No understanding. I guess the threat to them of litigation and the possible loss of their positions within the Church and school prohibited them from communicating with me about this.

The threatening party still works there, but I could be sacrificed. She's a Catholic in good standing.

"I'm sorry that happened to you."

"Me too," she nodded.

Then, she reached over and gave me a big hug. "Thank you for lunch," she said. "And thank you for calling today."

She sat back in her seat and paused for a moment.

"The Church has such an opportunity," she said. "But it's so far behind in its willingness to be real and human and related. We go to a church now, and it really is possible. The celebration, the ceremony, the people, the sermon—every aspect of the experience is real and related and applicable to my life today.

"They have such an opportunity," she repeated.

She opened the door and got out. She held the door open and put her head into the truck to look at me.

"The worse part of it, of everything that happened, was afterwards. There I was sitting across the dinner table from the man who raped me. As if nothing happened."

She closed the door and walked to the building.

Her voice stayed with me the rest of the day. *As if nothing happened.* After work, I stopped for a coffee and wrote a rough draft of this story. That same evening, sometime around 9pm, she texted me, thanking me again for our lunch and our earlier conversation.

I called her up and asked her if I could read to her what I had just written.

She listened.

Then, we talked about some things—I don't remember.

At one point before we hung up, she said, "As you were reading to me, I was moved to tears. I was experiencing the deep and real passage of time. Like I had lived and grown and could look back with wisdom. It was slow and powerful and unexpected. Thank you very much. It resonated inside of me in a way I couldn't avoid.

"And then," she continued, "when you were done reading, you began talking about something else. Something unrelated to this thing you had just written, this gift you had just given me. I still had tears in my eyes. I just wasn't done yet. I wasn't ready to move on."

Briefly, I thought I could have anticipated how the written story would affect her. Maybe I should have just let the experience settle into my memory. Maybe it wasn't my story to tell. And then I remembered what she'd said earlier—*we're all broken somehow*—and I decided to humbly appreciate her generosity.

The Liar

At the end of the day, I'm lying on the living room couch half asleep, hanging onto the edge of consciousness—my fingers losing their grip. The TV is on. Millionaire is starting and The Simpsons just ended. The kids are laughing. It must be 9pm.

"Hey, get ready for bed you guys," I say into the living room without opening my eyes. Oh, I'm so tired. Wish someone would pick me up, carry me to bed and tuck me in.

"Hurry up," I say with a little more agitation in my voice. "Let's go. Get ready."

I don't hear them scuffling toward the bathroom, so I squint open my eyes and they're still sitting on the floor facing the television screen. They're stiff and staring, as if poised to win the big one—three prairie dogs propped up to see what's going on.

"HEY!" I yell. "Get going NOW!"

I stay facing them and keep my eyes open long enough to see them get up and walk toward the bathroom. Then, I roll back over and melt into the couch again. I'm so damn tired.

The water goes on and off in the bathroom. The kids are brushing their teeth. The older two are moving quickly now. They bump into each other in the hallway, and they laugh and giggle, playing like I'm mad and they'd better hurry.

"Get going, Patrick," I yell down the hall to our youngest. "Get in bed!"

Regis asks about the name of the offensive position next to the center in football, for $8,000. That's easy. It's the guard. And the guy chooses linebacker. That's defense. I should go on that show.

Then, drool from my mouth catches my attention and wakes me up. I roll toward the TV, and Regis asks a lady if she really wants to use her third lifeline for this one. Apparently, Regis knows the answer, and she doesn't.

I wipe the drool from my mouth and try to get my bearings. The clock over the mantle reads 9:43pm. I wonder where my wife, Sara, is. She's usually home from karate by nine. She didn't wake me if she came in while I was sleeping. She's not here.

Down the hallway, a muttering of words sounds like Patrick. His light is still on. I know I should get up and see how he's doing. But, I don't want to get up. I'm tired, and I'm not moving. So, I yell down the hall instead.

"Patrick! Get into bed. And turn the damn light off."

"I would," his voice answered. "If you wouldn't lie to me."

"What do you mean, *Lie to you*?" I say. "Get to bed, and be quiet. NOW!"

The couch is comfortable. I should get up and see what he means. Plus, Sara's going to be home any minute, and the kids aren't asleep yet. But, I don't want to get up.

"Patrick, are you in bed, yet?" I yell down the hallway.

"You don't have to yell at me." He sniffles and mumbles.

What's he talking about? Lie to him? I think to myself, and go over the events of the evening. I've just been laying here, doing nothing really. I didn't lie to him.

"I didn't lie to you," I say down the hallway.

"Yes! You! Did!" He responds. "I just don't want you to lie to me."

"What are you talking about? I didn't lie to you." I'm thinking as fast as I can, and I'm tired and I don't want to get up, and Sara's coming home. What's he talking about?

"Go to bed, Patrick. Turn the light out. It's way past your bedtime."

It's way past my bedtime, I'm thinking. And I roll over to watch Regis, again. I consider going to see Patrick, but the Fastest Finger question is something I know. BDCA. Yeah! Got it. I should go in this show.

Just then, Sara walks in with bags of groceries hanging from her fingers.

"All the lights are on?" she says.

"Yeah," I say, "I dropped dead on the couch, and I haven't been able to get up."

She looks down the hallway and sees Patrick's light on. I turn and look. Before I can say anything, Patrick says out again through his sniffles, "I don't know why you have to lie to me, Dad?"

She looks at me. We put the groceries down in the kitchen. She takes her karate jacket off and asks, "What's he talking about?"

"I don't know. I told them to get ready for bed, and he's been moving real slow. So, for the past half hour he's been saying I lied to him. I don't know what he's talking about."

"YOU LIED!" Patrick shouts forcefully from his bedroom.

"We . . . had . . . a . . . deal," he cries.

"You said," he continues, "you'd tell me before you were going to yell at me. But tonight, you just started yelling."

"He's right, you know," Sara says. She moves into the kitchen and leaves me there.

Damn. He is right. Damn, damn, damn. My eyes are wide open now.

A couple of weeks back, I had yelled at him. He had a deep-felt reaction and cried profusely. I realized his response to me was something other than defiance, so I asked him what was up. He told me it scared him sometimes when I yell, that it can be surprising and frightening for him. I told him I didn't intend to frighten him, only to get him moving in the right direction.

We agreed that I needed to yell every once in a while—that would be alright. Maybe we could find a way that wouldn't be frightening for him. We discovered that if he knew I was getting mad and going to yell, then he wouldn't be frightened.

That was our deal, then. I would warn him before I yelled. And our agreement worked until now. Over the past weeks, whenever Patrick didn't respond to my initial request, and I felt a need to raise my voice, I'd warn him that I was about ready to yell. And in each instance, he got the message before I said another word, and he responded promptly to my request.

But tonight, I was tired and lazy and I just started yelling. He's right. I lied to him.

"Patrick," I say down the hallway. "Please, come out here. I need to talk to you."

He pokes his head out into the hallway. I nod my head and gesture for him to come over to me. He walks down the hall, sliding his feet slowly behind him. As he gets closer, he lowers his eyes and looks at the floor. He knows it's late and past his bedtime.

"Patrick," I say, "You're right."

His eyes rise up to meet mine. He stands tall and looks directly into my eyes.

"I forgot about our agreement," I continue. "Tonight, I was tired and lazy, and I didn't take time to warn you that I was going to yell."

He nods his head up and down.

"Did I frighten you?"

He keeps nodding.

"Patrick, I didn't mean to scare you."

"I know, Dad."

"And I'm sorry I forgot about our deal."

He's nodding, and he's looks like he's all done with the conversation. He's relaxed and ready to go.

"You tired?" I ask him.

He nods.

"Go give your Mom a hug and kiss. Then, I'll put you to bed."

He scampers into the kitchen, gives Sara a big embrace and returns to me. I pick him up into my arms and carry him into his room and over to his bed. I lay him down and pull the covers up to his chin. He smiles.

"Let's say prayers," he says.

We say our litany, and he finishes with ". . . and thank you, God, for the very, very, very best Mommy and the very, very, very best Daddy. Amen."

Before I get up to leave his room, I brush back the hair on his forehead and say, "Patrick, thank you for reminding me tonight about our deal. You can tell me when you think something is unfair like that. You have to know, though, that some time you just have to do what I ask you to do. Whether I yell or not."

"I know dad." He was clear.

I turn off the light and look back to see him. He's facing the wall, and his eyes are closed.

I meet up with Sara in the kitchen.

"Whoa," I breathe a big breath.

"How do you like that, Dad?" she says.

"He was right."

"You bet he was."

She puts her arms around my neck and smiles.

The Old Man Beside Me

My Grandma died last week. Now, both my Grandpa and my Grandma are gone. I remember when I was young and they used to come down from Northern California to visit us. Grandma always sat at the kitchen table with us and played cards—500 Rummy or Hearts. She loved to win. And she was hard to beat.

Grandpa would go into San Pedro and buy fresh yellowtail at the docks and get sourdough from his cousin Ante's restaurant. Before dinner, we'd all sit at the table, and he cooked, drinking red wine and telling stories of the orchards where my Mom grew up. Mom would remember. Her eyes would drift off somewhere, and she'd smile. Sometimes she'd laugh out loud—so fresh, and so good to hear her laughter.

He always drank red wine.

Three years ago, I asked my Mom about Grandpa—whether she thought about him much anymore. A few days later, she called me from her work. Her voice was different, though. It wasn't the *Feed-the-dog-Do-the-dishes-Could-you-pick-up-some-groceries* voice that I was used to. I was still living at home and finishing college at the local university.

"Oh, I'm glad I caught you," she said. "But don't you have school today?"

"Yeah," I said. "I'm leaving in a minute."

"You asked about Grandpa yesterday," and then she paused as though I knew what she was thinking.

"I've been thinking about it," she continued. "It's kind of strange."

"I don't know," I said. "I've just been thinking about him a lot. Like every time I use a knife in the kitchen, I use his old one. The short one with the broken wood handle. It's like I have to use it, even though it's a little dull."

As I was telling her this, she'd "uh-huh" after every sentence, as if she knew what I was going to say before I was finished.

"Well, that's interesting," she said, "because I just got off the phone with Grandma, and she's really having a tough time of it. Seems we all have Grandpa on our minds. It's been a few years, and I think she's finally allowing herself to grieve over his death."

The three of us had Grandpa in us. I liked that. We were all connected that way, and it was nice. He was off somewhere holding us together.

"She's not feeling well, and she asked me to visit her for a week. I think she wants some company." Mom spoke slow and definite, like the words were stopped up in her throat.

"Is she alright?"

"I hope so," she said. "She's never asked me to visit before. Almost as if she needs me there. It's just not like her."

"When are you leaving?"

"I won't be able to get out of here until Saturday morning. And then I'll just have to see how things go, I guess."

"I have to run, Mom," I said, "or I'll miss my class. I'm already gonna be late. I'll be home early tonight."

When I hung up the phone, I felt sad that Grandma had asked Mom to visit. I was glad Mom was going, but it just didn't sound good to me. And I didn't want to think of losing my Grandma. But, what was so dire about an aging woman asking her daughter to visit her?

The week before she left, Mom looked worried and kept herself busy. Then every day that she was gone, I'd ask Dad about Grandma. I knew he was keeping in touch.

"How's Grandma?" I'd ask.

He'd say, "Not too well. Keep praying." We didn't talk much.

Mom stayed two weeks and, when she came home, she told everyone that Grandma was fine. I was relieved. I didn't want Mom to hurt.

Three years ago, I knew Mom was scared. But after Grandma died last week, Mom stood tall and responded as someone in the family is expected to. She got busy making plans and arranging flights. She spent a whole afternoon and evening calling everyone, telling them what had happened and when and where the rosary and funeral were.

I heard her say things like, "Nothing, really. Just prayers, thank you."

I think the years helped prepare her. She accepted condolences yesterday at Grandma's funeral, and I was proud of her. She had a regal presence to her. She hugged the huggers and shook hands with those who were more comfortable with that. She received her friends and family where they were, and she didn't impose her grief on them.

People came to the house all afternoon, bringing cakes and casseroles, staying for a cup of coffee or a glass of wine. It was a long day. Somewhere near nine last night, Mom and Dad and I were sitting in the living room listening to the silence. Mom looked straight ahead. Dad and I looked at her then at each other. Mom got up, and Dad followed her into their bedroom. They closed the door.

I got tired, put my head back and fell asleep. At five this morning, I woke wide awake, still sitting on the couch and with the lights still on. I was hungry. I didn't want to start something in the kitchen and risk waking Mom up. She was exhausted, and I hoped she'd sleep in most of the morning. Closing my eyes, I thought I'd try to sleep until later. But I was hungry. I got up and turned off the lights and went out the front door.

The Parasol was the only restaurant open that early. I drove down the empty boulevard and turned into the parking lot, surprised to see so many cars. I parked facing the street and saw three delivery trucks whip up the gutter leaves as they passed under the street light.

The Parasol was busy. The booths were mostly filled, and the counter was crowded. I had to slip into a seat between two guys, an old man to my right and a thick trucker on my other side. The trucker was reading the morning paper, and I looked over at the headlines.

"The Grandchildren of the '60s," it read. In the picture, a middle-aged woman wrapped her arms around a young musician. He held a white electric guitar. The caption said she "shares a love of '60s rock 'n' roll with her 24 year old son."

I ordered my breakfast, and then I looked around. It seemed that everyone knew everyone else. I didn't know anyone. The waitresses talked and laughed with their customers. I could hardly believe there was this much bustling activity at 5am anywhere. Most of the clientele were grey-haired, and I wondered if these customers all came from Leisure World, the retirement community down the road.

One waitress wore blue make-up around her eyes, and she had high, red cheeks. The make-up thickened as she got closer and walked past me. Closer up, her make-up didn't adequately mask her wrinkles and her age, but I guessed she wanted it to. I watched her start a new pot of coffee.

Two of the waitresses looked like sisters, and I said to the old man beside me, "Those two sisters?"

"No," he said. "That one there. She's Miss Missouri. And the other one's Texas. That's where they're from. They're good girls. Good service here."

"Yeah, they're quick," I said as Texas set my spinach omelette down in front of me. I started right in and didn't stop until I'd put a dent in my appetite. Then, I sat back and relaxed, sipping coffee and picking bites here and there.

The old man beside me turned my way and said, "Quite an appetite."

"Yeah," I said. "I'm hungry."

We nodded at each other, drinking coffee.

"I've got a grandson eats like that."

I took another bite. Then, I turned toward him so he'd know I was listening.

"He's big. Six foot one and a hundred, eighty-five. He's just fifteen."

"That's pretty big," I said.

"He wants to play football. I was showing him how to golf the other week, and he can hit. Farther than me."

"Was it straight, though?" I asked.

"Yeah, pretty much," he said, and he put his coffee mug out where Texas filled it up. Then, she filled mine.

"I think he's going to be a football player," he said. "I've got three grandsons. The one that's fifteen, though, he's the biggest one."

I thought about telling him that, if his grandson was fifteen and wanted to play football, he should be on his high school team by now and he should be training hard for next season. If he really wanted to play, he'd be working out and running and doing all the . . .

And then it occurred to me that maybe these were Grandpa's hopes and dreams. Maybe Grandson didn't want to play football at all. This old man sat next me in this restaurant, and he was talking to a stranger about the boys in his life—his grandsons. What was more likely, I thought, was that he didn't know what his grandsons wanted to be. Maybe he was confusing a conversation he'd had when the boy was younger with the size the boy is now.

His eyes followed Texas as she carried an order from behind the counter to one of her booths across the diner. When she began setting the plates down, he said, "He's just fifteen, but that boy eats like you do. I watched you here, and I couldn't eat all that in three days."

He turned back to drink his coffee. His check, the only thing in front of him, was face down.

I then remembered standing at the side of my Grandpa's bed one day when he was old and frail. He reached out and held my hand with both of his thin, bony hands. His bottom hand held mine like a handshake. His top hand caressed my hand as we talked. Without letting go of the handshake, he reached over with his top hand and picked up a book from his nightstand. He offered the book to me and pointed to a small slip of paper that was marking a page.

I opened the book and read the title of the chapter beginning on that page: *Writing From The Heart.*

"Take it," he said. "It's for you."

This gesture from my Grandpa surprised me. I hadn't known that he had noticed much about me until then.

I got up to pay the cashier for my breakfast. When I returned to my place at the counter, I stood behind my seat and leaned over and placed an old limp dollar bill next to my empty plate. I collected my keys off the counter and touched the old man so he'd know I was going.

Putting my hand on his shoulder, I said, "It was nice talking with you. Have a good one, now."

He lifted his coffee mug and nodded. I turned to leave and behind me I heard him say, "You take care." Looking back, I saw him smiling at me and nodding.

Feeling heavy and full, I went out the doors of The Parasol into a morning that was not yet awake. It was almost dark and almost light. I walked through the cool morning air to my car, unlocked the door and eased myself onto the seat. I sat and watched the sun crawl up to the Mobil sign across the street until it peeped over, splashing into my eyes. I had to look away.

I flipped the visor down on the windshield to block the light and sat there, looking at cars and thinking. I sat there and thought about Grandma not being around. Maybe I should've gone and visited her more, or written, or something. I thought about how Mom must feel, her Mom gone.

I stared, just stared as the cars passed, thinking that my Mom was going to die someday. I stared as the cars passed, and my eyes burned. I just stared, and the tears rolled down my cheeks.

The Legacy

My Dad and I are at breakfast early. I'm on my way to the shop, and this is his favorite breakfast spot. Mine too, for work mornings—Paul's serves fast, full meals at remarkable prices. They always have a $2.99 special, and I rarely finish everything on my plate. The coffee is self-serve. I get up and serve my Dad his second cup. Before returning the pot to its warmer on the counter, I top off every cup in the place. People are smiling and raising their cups. This is something my Dad always does.

We're spending time. He's heading to his office, the opposite direction of my shop. We used to meet here often. Now, this is a special morning when our schedules have us both available. We're just sitting here, drinking our coffee, long pauses between the words.

He says something about the Fantasy Football League he's in with my brother. Sam picked a pretty good team. They're in third, and last week they scored some long plays and big points.

"Tell me something," he says. "Something I can't figure out. Maybe you know." He puts his cup down and looks at it. "I can't figure out why Sam would fire Steve." He spins his mug around a full circle. "I just can't figure it out. Steve's a hard worker." He thinks for a moment. "Maybe I should ask him myself."

"Well, yeah," I say abruptly. "I know why." He looks at me, surprised the answer is so obvious. "Sam and I talked about it a month ago. I told him he was going to fire him."

"But, why?"

"Dad, Sam's like you and me. We have expectations of people in our lives." I feel momentum building inside me. "And we don't explain what we want."

I know I should shut up, but I keep going. "He did what you and I always do. We think people can read our minds, and we make them wrong for not knowing what we're thinking. Then, we kill them off."

The warm morning welcome disappears from his face. He looks at me and tilts his head like he doesn't know what I'm saying. Or maybe it's that he doesn't want to participate with me. But I know what I'm saying. I've been saying it for thirty-five years, trying to find the words to talk about what I'm seeing without driving him away. The accumulating years rush up to meet me, and I continue talking—for the ten thousandth time, like a rolling train out of control.

"Dad, we all do the same thing. Then, we're some kind of confused about the wreckage we leave behind. How people don't know we love them. That they have some weirdness about our tone, or our loudness, or that we don't listen. We know what we want, but people around us don't know how to respond. I do it, too. Look at all the people you hired and fired. And I've done it at the shop. It's amazing you and I are still married."

He says, "I don't know how this applies to Sam and Steve."

"Of course, you don't." I'm unconscious now, and my mouth is open, and someone should take a baseball bat to my head. I'm on a downhill slide, and I don't know how to stop myself.

"You never know how it relates," I continue. "You just go along and everyone else should adjust to you. You don't know how anyone else is doing, really. Because you don't ask. And then you're surprised that some of us aren't getting what we want from you. Like you're not responsible for your relationships."

I listened finally to what I was saying and realized I wasn't explaining anything to him. I was ready to give up trying.

"But," my Dad says, "Steve's a really hard worker."

"Dad, you don't get it." I'm sliding again. "It doesn't matter. We do this. We kill people off. It's your legacy."

The last word hangs there. I don't say anything for a long while. Then, like a sink backing up and all the wet garbage surfacing, I hate myself again. This isn't what I wanted to tell him. I did it again. I turned a perfectly nice time with my Dad into an ugly self-portrait, and I launched that ugliness right at him.

I don't know how to get out of this conversation. I avoid my last sentence and return, instead, to what he said.

"Dad, Sam and I talked about this a while back. He thought he was being clear with Steve about his expectations. And maybe he was. I don't know."

Someone comes over to our table and offers to top off our mugs.

We both decline. Time to get to work. We stand up. I lean over and kiss him on the cheek. We go out the door to our separate cars into our different days.

Legacy? What was I thinking? I didn't want to bring that up, or to have a child's reaction. Haven't I gotten any further than this? Who am I to talk to him like that? What an arrogant SOB!

I'm driving to work drowning in the ugly realization that, for all the ground I've gained in my life, I can't get away from my ego long enough to let my Dad know how much I love him. *I just wanted him to know I love him*, I keep repeating to myself. The drive is a short one, and the workday quickly swallows my attention.

The next day, my parents leave for Tennessee to visit my older brother for two and a half weeks. They don't need me to take them to the airport. They'll let me know if they need me to pick them up.

Over the next two weeks, I consider calling my Dad, explaining myself, apologizing. But, I just don't know what else to say. He probably won't even remember what I said. Maybe I should wait until he gets back from Tennessee, be with him face to face—and just be with him. Relax and let him know how important he is to me. But, how do I do that? I always tell him I love him. I hug him every time I see him. But, I'm not sure he gets how important he is in my life. So, I think about this every day for two weeks, and I pray he's safe arriving home so I can have another conversation with him.

That word *legacy* keeps knocking on my door. What is his legacy?

The inquiry stays with me each day, during work and at home. At work, I am noticing my effect on my employees. At home, I am watching my kids interact. I'm listening to my wife. My wife and I go to parent-teacher conferences at the school, and all three teachers thank us for sharing our children with them. I ask each teacher what we can do at home to support their efforts, and they say keep doing more of the same. I have private moments with each of my children, and they are warm and kind and appreciative. They are expressive and generous with their love for me.

Generous. I think about that word. I have not been generous with my Dad. Of all the people in my life, I have been least generous with him. I have accepted that it was okay for me to be resigned and out of contact with him.

Slowly, over the days, his legacy begins to reveal itself to me. It's always been there, every day of my life. But, I've been too busy being critical and demanding to appreciate it. As I consider the awesome breadth of his impact, I become calm and peaceful and so filled with the thought of him that I'm tearful in unlikely moments.

My parents return home from Tennessee, and they don't need me to pick them up at the airport.

The next week, I'm hustling around the shop when my Dad walks through the front door. He hands me a packet of photographs. They're shots of my five year old son's soccer team, of which I am the coach. He came to a game a month ago, and took these snapshots.

"Keep them. They're yours," he says.

"Come on into the office," I say. "Have a seat."

Just then, someone hands me a phone, and I walk off into the other room to answer the caller's question. I quickly remove myself from the call, and return to my Dad. But, he's halfway out the door, waving goodbye to my employees. I follow him out the door, and ask him about Tennessee. Tennessee was great, and my brother's doing fine, and my Dad starts to get into his car.

I reach my hand out across his car's open doorway to block his way. He looks at me.

"Dad, I've been wanting to talk with you."

"What is it?"

"Well," I start slowly. "Before you left for Tennessee, we were at breakfast, and I said something to you that wasn't very kind. I've been thinking about it, and I wanted to say I'm sorry."

"It mustn't have been that bad, because I don't remember it."

"I do," I say, and I look away from him. "Dad, we were at breakfast at Paul's, and you asked me about Sam firing Steve, and I said something about the way we are and that that's your legacy."

He remembers. The moment I say the word *legacy*, there is a faint glint of recognition in his eye. Sadness, really.

"I was wrong, Dad, and mean. That really isn't your legacy at all. I've been thinking about you every day. And I know what your legacy is."

"You do?" He says, jokingly. "Good, because I haven't got a clue."

I look into his eyes and say, "Your legacy is Kelsey, and James Dobbins."

"I pray for those kids every day."

"I know you do," and there's recognition between us. Kelsey was the four year old girl who lived with me, my wife and children while her mother was rehabbing her drug addiction. James was the kindergartener I was a Big Brother to while attending college.

"Dad," I continue, "I remember growing up and all the cousins when they came over to visit. Their experience they had in our home was nothing they got anywhere else. You were the Man in our home, and it made a difference for them to experience you that way. They were visibly impacted by you." My cousins all came from divorced homes, and my parents are still married after 40 years.

"It was good for them," he says.

"I know it was." I continue, "I remember when the Hoach's came to live with us, Hong and his parents. And when Fred spent the season in our home." Hong and his parents were Vietnamese refugees who lived with my family while I was growing up—until they became self-sufficient. We drove down to Camp Pendleton in the station wagon and brought them to our home. Fred was from Texas and on my college football team. He needed a place to stay, and my Dad offered our home.

"Dad, people were always coming to our home. I could bring anyone home who needed a place to stay, and I knew it would be okay. It was just understood. And people liked being there. We were a good place to be. Our meals were parties."

He's listening to me.

"I remember going with you to the convalescent homes to visit. I hated going because of the smell. But, they all knew you because you went every week and you knew their names, and you'd introduce me, and they'd reach their hands out over the sides of their beds to touch me. I'd hold their bony hands, and you'd go off to the next room to visit somebody else. You'd leave me alone in there with them, and I knew you just wanted to visit the next person, to give as many lonely, old people the warmth of a visit.

"Your Legacy, Dad, is that you have seven grown children in the world who at any moment open their doors and share their abundance with the less fortunate. I see it. I talk to them, and you created that in the world. Like you have seven satellite offices operating with love and generosity in the world. And then there's all the grandkids. They are each phenomenal."

He looks at me. There is invitation in his eyes. He is standing in the moment and receiving.

"Dad, I love you very much."

"You have no idea how much I love you." He bear hugs me. "Every one of you guys. I'm so blessed."

"You created it."

We look at each other. He reaches and puts his hand on the top of his open car door. Slowly, he eases into the driver's seat. He closes the door and starts the car. He rolls down his window.

"Have a great day," he says.

"I am," I nod my head.

He pulls out and drives off.

Flowers Removed Every Thursday

Today is Friday, and Mia buried her grandfather today. She's five years old and will be in kindergarten in the Fall. She's the second youngest of Frank's four daughters. Frank and I went to high school together, and he's the kind of man who gets into your heart and resides there like a brother. I'm always glad to see him and this day, I knew, would be difficult.

An hour earlier in the church, Frank delivered his father's eulogy. He's the youngest of five children, and he spoke of his father with poise, humor, love and admiration. I listened thinking of how proud his father must be.

I don't know Mia all that well. She told me about school and her age after I lifted her up into my arms. I was standing in the cemetery then, back from the graveside gathering of friends and Frank's Italian family. His father's casket was still elevated above the artificial grass carpet. Frank, his mother and his siblings were hugging those around them—now lining up for a few moments of face-to-face condolences.

Mia had wandered to the back of the group. She was looking down at the gravestones then looking up at the people towering around her. She saw me across a short distance of grass and walked slowly my way. She paused, looked at a gravestone, stared at a tall man in suit and tie, looked back toward her grandfather's casket then up to the backs of a few women in sundresses.

Her own flowery dress and curled hair were the result of her mother's careful attention to detail. Mia appeared comfortable with her distance from the gathering, and I thought it might be because I was standing there. Frank had texted me after I had dinner at their house a few months ago. He wrote that Mia said, "I like Mr. BigMaster who came over the house."

She wandered over toward me and almost bumped into a young couple attending to their daughter's grave. I looked up and saw Frank next to his mother, and Frank's wife was with their other girls. If either of them looked my way, I wanted to let them know that Mia was okay and that she was being looked after.

The couple behind Mia approached earlier during the service and knelt down at a grave just behind Frank's group. The mother carried a colorful bouquet of fresh wildflowers, and the father carried an assortment of supplies that included a battery-powered set of shears. The mother wiped to a shiny gleam the charcoal-black granite gravestone with a wet paper towel, and the father trimmed the grass that shaped their daughter's rectangular gravesite. He trimmed everything—around the edges of the gravestone and around the circular edges of each of three in-ground vases dug for their flowers. The mother cut the flower stems to size and arranged them into the vase-inserts her husband filled with water.

They were sitting back on the grass now looking relaxed; their knees just at the edge of their daughter's grave. Their private homage was neither interrupted nor deterred by the proximate crowd around Mia's grandfather. The dates under their girl's name were 1984-1998. Eleven years ago, I thought. She was fourteen years old.

Mia was wandering. She wasn't heading exactly to me. She didn't see the couple. Her back was to them, and she stepped in their direction a few times in slow motion until she stood directly on their daughter's grave. She didn't realize they were there. She wouldn't know why.

They both looked up at me and smiled.

"Gracias, pero todo esta bien," the mother said, nodding to let me know she was at ease and comfortable with Mia's presence.

I was uncomfortable, though, and tried to alert Mia to her intrusion. She looked at me as I approached her and reached up to my arms. I picked her up and held her to my chest. She rested her head on my shoulder, and I stepped away from the girl's gravesite.

When I turned back toward Frank, the mother and father were both staring blankly at their daughter's grave. Frank caught my eye across the distance between us and over the heads of those around him. He smiled, satisfied in his need to know where Mia was.

"Are you okay?" I asked her.

She lifted her head and looked at me. Then, she nodded, and her curly hair reminded me of a young Shirley Temple.

"Would you like to get down, or would you like to stay up here?"

"I would like to stay up here," she said.

"You know, your Dad and I went to high school together?"

"I know that," she said, smiling.

From her perch up in my arms, she looked around—first at her family and friends, locating both her parents. Then, she looked toward the ground at the various headstones lined in rows across the top of the grass. I tried to follow her gaze. When she tired of looking around, she looked at me.

I stepped aside and revealed the headstone that was nearest me. It was of a friend of mine. She was married to another high school friend and classmate of ours. Earlier, walking toward Frank's family from my parked car, I recognized this as the site of her burial and was surprised that she was so close to Frank's father. I had been standing back from the group to be near Celeste's grave. She died valiantly fighting non-Hodgkin's lymphoma fourteen years before.

Mia and I both turned and looked down.

"This is where we buried my friend, Celeste," I told her. "She was your Dad's friend, too."

Mia had sadness all over her face. Maybe this was too much.

"It's hard to say goodbye to people we love," I continued. Then, I turned her with me back to see her family around her grandfather's casket. I worried that this was all so heavy for her. It was heavy for me. I tried to find something else to talk about.

"How old are you?"

"I just turned five."

"You did? When was your birthday?"

"June 10th."

Two weeks ago, I thought.

"Do you start kindergarten this next year?"

"Yes," she said, nodding.

"Are you excited to start school?"

She shrugged her shoulders and squinted her eyes. I couldn't guess if she was nervous about starting school or if maybe she thought it was a weird question.

"Well, when I was your age, I was nervous to start kindergarten."

She smiled.

"But, don't do what I did."

She squinted her eyes again.

"On my very first day of kindergarten, I wet my pants."

She smiled, and her eyes opened wide.

"I did," I continued. "I was sitting in the classroom and the teacher was talking and I didn't want to interrupt her. I was in the very last seat behind everyone else, and I needed to go to the bathroom. But I was scared to raise my hand and ask. I waited too long and peed my pants right there in my seat."

Maybe I shouldn't have told her that.

"So, when you get to school, be sure to raise your hand and ask any question you need to."

She smiled and nodded.

I stood there for a while longer. The expansive cemetery was green all around. And mostly quiet, except for the bagpipes a hundred yards behind us. The piper was in full plaid regalia, standing in the shade under a tree beside a family of five gathered graveside. The aching pipes had been wailing in the background all morning.

Between us, white doves pecked and fluttered. They seemed to hover around a particular area. I counted eight on the ground and five in the air veering like a boomerang back to the others.

Mia's grandfather was being buried at the curved end of a horseshoe-shaped roadway that traveled through the grounds. Cars were parked on both sides of the roadway, and there were no parking spaces left available. Frank's group had gathered simultaneously with another family just across the road.

I hadn't noticed much about this family across the road until they stood still and faced Frank's family, frozen. At one point in our service, two military men draped an American flag over the top of Mia's grandfather's casket. They stood erect facing each other at either end of the casket. The soldier closest to Frank's mother turned toward her and explained what was about to happen. He explained the appreciation our country had for her husband's service in the military. He described the significance of his salute and the historical nature of the song *Taps* and why we would soon hear the bugler who had inconspicuously set up just off to the side of us, away from the crowd.

The bugler was at attention in the hot sun, his bugle tucked under his arm, his instrument's case empty next to him on the grass.

The lead sergeant addressed the rest of us now. Veterans and anyone currently in the military were asked to stand at attention in full salute. The rest of us were asked to stand respectfully with our hands over our hearts.

Then, *Taps* began. The bugler was nearby, and his cry was loud and reaching and resonant. The bagpipes wafted in and out behind the bugler. No one moved.

Staring at Mia's grandfather's casket and the flag and the soldiers, I wondered how many times a week (or a day) they marched and stood to honor the service of a fellow soldier they had not known. Past them and across the road to the other side of the horseshoe, the family across the road stopped their service. I loved their salute. Every member of their group turned toward Mia's grandfather, their hands over their hearts. A few of the older men raised their chins and saluted from their foreheads.

They were a smaller group than ours. And I noticed none of the men wore suits. Few wore ties. Some wore cowboy boots and bolo ties. Many were dressed in big, oversized white t-shirts and baggy jeans. The women dressed in high heels and tight dresses. Their faces were made up as if they were going dancing on a Saturday night.

Their priest stood next to the woman closest to their casket. She wore a long, black dress with long sleeves. She also wore a veil that covered her entire head, face and neck. She, too, turned our direction and stood in silent salute with Frank's family while *Taps* played its every note.

No one moved.

After the last note played, silence.

The lead sergeant faced Mia's grandfather and very deliberately, with the help of the soldier at the other end of the casket, folded the United States flag into a triangle precisely the way we had in grade school folded notebook paper to play paper football across our desks. He took his time and tucked each fold as he went. When the entire flag was tightly packaged, he handed it to Frank's mother and saluted her. His associate marched up to stand beside him. They turned on a dime and marched directly to the bugler who was standing with his instrument packed in its case by his side. One by one they turned and marched to their cars and departed.

Both families stood still until the job was completed.

Now, with Mia in my arms, I wondered how this had all affected her.

"How is your heart?" I asked her.

"My heart hurts," she said, looking into my eyes.

"Yes, this hurts," I said. "You miss your Papa," and Mia nodded her head.

Earlier at the church, I had heard Frank's wife refer to his father this way while speaking to her girls.

"Mia," I continued, "your Papa's in your heart . . ."

She smiled.

"And everyone who meets you will know your Papa because they know you . . . and because you love your Papa so much. He lives in your heart."

Her smile widened.

I looked over, and the crowd around Frank thinned out. Friends walked across the grass to their cars, on their way to lay out the food and drinks for the reception to be held in one of the few buildings down at the other end of the cemetery.

"Mia, today I'm celebrating your Papa. And all these people here are celebrating his life also. The bagpipes and the doves," I turned to show her the man in the kilt under the trees. We looked at the doves, still fluttering.

When I turned back, Frank and his wife were smiling and standing right near us. Mom was checking to see that Mia was comfortable, and Frank stepped closer to wrap us both up in his arms.

"I love you, man," he said. His eyes were misty and, besides the obvious, I was holding in my arms a very precious joy in his life.

"We are celebrating Mia's Papa," I said to them. They nodded. Then, I said to Mia, "All those people across the road stopped to salute your Papa when the bugler played his tune."

A Navy veteran, this struck Frank in his heart and he gasped when he heard this. He looked across the road to the other family. Mia laid her head into my shoulder and rolled out of my arms toward her mother.

"This is Celeste's," Frank said, looking down near my feet. Our friend and classmate had lost his wife years before many of us had given any thought to losing our aging parents. Frank's father would be resting less than thirty feet from Celeste.

"You know," Frank paused, "Celeste was my Confirmation partner." He was still looking down at her engraved name. I hadn't known that he knew her from grade school.

After a few long, quiet moments, we turned toward our cars, and I told Frank I would not be attending the reception. It was Friday, and I had been on vacation all week. I needed to get to the office and make sure payroll was handled. We bear-hugged and promised to see each other soon.

I drove around the horseshoe toward the exit. On the last block of grass before the driveway, an obvious, white wooden sign rose from the lawn: *"Flowers Removed Every Thursday."*

POEMS

Hollow . . .

Tears trickle
down the inside wall,

drip, drop into
an empty puddle
of me.

Intimacy.

Like kittens
we paw the ball of string
until a claw catches hold.

Then, we shake to get free
and scamper away.

Night Rain.

Tiny soldiers
mobbishly march on my roof,
some nudged off the edge,

others forced against my window,

rushing to find shelter
before the morning light
exposes their position.

6 am

Alarm
rattles me
to consciousness.

I reach over your side
and hit the snooze

then flop down
on the empty space
where you would be
if you were here.

Memorex.

When Susan sings
her words weave through the sheer-curtain sunset,
her music wets the walls.

My wandering emotions,
dancing over stockpiled laundry,
are pulled to the peaks
and rolled through the pastures
of her vocal landscape.

Her huge voice then whispers down
to the point of a needle,
disappearing into the warm silence
of an echoing heartbeat.

The Silent Vantage Point.

Full moon morning sky
Dusted powder blue
Whisper soft a memory
Sunshine fire through

Flatten wide the reverie
Melt the wax and flame
And flesh traverse
The rocks and harsh terrain

Full the silent vantage point
Steps plodding in the sand
Sweat slips down the ravine
Steps swept across the land

Prairie sounds are sunset blue
Dusty red and dry
Windblown afterthought
Guitar solo sky

Fire-cracked kindling
Shadow mountain grey
Listening for the yellow moon
In the disappearing day

And shadows vanish darkening
A sky of scattered light
And silence howls
Its homage to the night

The Opening.

A rose unwraps herself
revealing her seclusion.

She knows the emptiness
enclosed in her confusion.

Slow opening is what she does
when drawn into unfolding

by tender confidences,
by being the beholden.

Old Friends.

Ask me to hold you
and I will.

Ask me to touch you
and I'd love to.

But ask for a kiss
and I wouldn't know
what to do.

Because I know the taste
of old friends . . .

Darts.

I must be hitting
unintended targets

for you to pin-point
fine marksmanship

when I'm just aimlessly
tossing words,

flying them one after the other
to keep you
at arms length.

Mirrors.

Forget me, please.
Then maybe I'll forget.

Forget me so that when I'm not thinking of you
you won't remind me to by thinking of me.

It works that way, you know.
I'm fine on my own.
Then, you see a sunset or the moon
or some other familiar part of us
and you think of me and I think of you.

You remind me to.
I know you do.

Forget me, please.

Where do you go?

A speck on the horizon,
a moment in the haze
just before you disappear
away from me.

Where do you go?

When I cannot see your shore,
adrift
and set off on my own,

my eyes reach for the sunset
for landmarks, flags
maybe a bird
flown from your harbor.

But there is nothing.

No smoke, no border
no margin of error.

Even clouds avoid me.

The Soft Blue Awakening.

I hear echoes of the questions
to the answers you sing
And I dance upon the music
to the songs you bring

And anticipate the sunrise
below midnight's largest eye
Until the soft blue awakening
dawns up the darkest sky

One day a word might rain down
drop upon a page I write
Inspired by the vista
and your ever-tender sight

Truth is the love I've known from you
has ever been the tune
The ocean in the background
as I've danced around the room

Self-Doubt.

I'm ten years old
standing in line for a roller coaster
that I have finally reached the height
to qualify to ride.

My nervous heart swells in my chest.
Slow, big breathing.
Watching the cars roll along.
Listening to the thunder under my feet.

On my toes,
I measure from my forehead
across to the line on the sign
that says I had to wait until now to ride.

I'm taller than the requirement, though.

And the thought occurs to me
that I could've ridden before today
if I had only found a way to get here.

The Factory.

Where do men come from?
Somewhere granite and bold, I guess.
Where do the shavings and edges shorn go
that made the men I know?

Where do boys go to learn
the dance daily for gold . . .
Numbers and values and how it all goes,
those rules every other man knows.

I'm not a very good man, I think . . .
cause where does all the sadness go,
and the fear and the wonder and the joy?
. . . Yet, I'm too big to be a boy.

Where do men come from?
And how do they get the feelings out?
Maybe someday I'll go and see
down at the man-making factory.

Dear Dad.

Went to the sea today
To see the waves roll away
Only to return and crash-splash my face
And salt-burn my eyes.

Went inside my heart today
And saw the you
I always knew
And tried to face the face I hate
But always wore to hate you more.

Went inside your heart today
To see the you
I never knew
And danced away the lonely years
In ocean spray and joyous tears.

A Mothers Valentine.
Mothers Pub, Sunset Beach.

After my third pinball, I go behind the bar to check everyone's drinks.
And Bill pushes his glass to me, "Fill me up."
I tilt his glass under the draft and pour up to an exact measure of foam.

A voice behind me bellows, "You work here? Where the hell you been?"
I turn to this guy and say, "What do you want?"
and his smoke reaches up burning my eyes.
Then, I get his Corona, get his change, and say, "No limes,"
thinking he's a jerk.

I walk back to my pinball game, hoping he leaves before my fifth ball.
Some of these guys sit on their stools
and suck their bottles forever.

After my game, I step over a dog's tail and hurry behind the bar
in time to smack a large cockroach
that tried to sneak behind the beer nuts.

The guy with the Corona is still here giving me his bad look.

The phone rings and I answer, "Mothers, can I help you?"
"Hi, Sweetie," she says, and I loosen up.
"Just called to say Happy Valentine's, and I love you."

"I love you, too," I say—meaning it.

After I hang up, I turn around and the guy with the Corona says,
"Who the hell's that?"

I just smile and say nothing.
"Some broad's got you whipped," he says.
Again, I smile with jelly in my eyes.

He looks down at his hand wrapped around his bottle.
Then, he lifts up the bottle, looks at me and nods,
and I nod in return.

After he drinks his beer, he almost smiles,
perhaps remembering what it is to be loved.

Occupation: Housewife

Destination: Unknown

I stand in the doorway facing the hot afternoon.
You just drove away. Didn't wave or glance back.
Just dropped off your set of keys and the final papers,
signed in triplicate.

The door open, I turn into the living room,
lean against the wall. There are no chairs.
No sofa. No furniture. Half-packed boxes.
A painting of mountains and a stream
crooked on the wall.
And carpet.

Wall-to-wall, walked on carpet disappears
under our bedroom door.
You didn't glance back. Just drove away.

Phone's ringing. Ringing. Ringing.
God. You just drove away.
Ringing. Ringing.

"Hello?"
"Yes. Mrs. Jenkins?"
"Uh huh."
*"This is Denise from The Realty Network, and our records show that your house
will enter the market at the end of the month. I'd like to set up an appointment
at your convenience, so we . . ."*
"Not today. Please. Not today.
I'll get in touch with you tomorrow."

Damn. I look at my home.
I walk to the front door and look out for a moment,
feel the afternoon heat.
I close the door and lock the dead-bolt.

Cafeteria Windows.

A hummingbird suspended
hangs in the air
vibrates in and out
of open petals

and me
in a lazy haze
of existence, tired
and still uneducated

yet quick enough to notice
the tiny fresh breeze
from the hummingbird's wings.

The Vicious Warriors.

You lean in the doorway
staring down at your feet
and I talk to the hair in your face.

A quick, wet glance
dares to check if I'm watching.

You don't hear what I'm saying—
too busy plotting your defenses,
stacking armies
against my offering.

I notice a battle inside you
but see no strategy
to combat the vicious warriors
in your mind.

Instead, you think I am the enemy.

As you fall apart
I count the casualties,
and from the perimeter
I stand watching fully equipped
and uninvited.

Tension.

A fly on the wall
saw it on the wall
cleaning itself

flew away into the window
wiggled down
to the sill
buzzing loud
louder
buzzing and bouncing

smacked it
paper wet with it

pinched its wing
picked it up
to see it
dead.

Autumn.

Tree tops,
erect in the wind,
penetrate the clouds
which own the sky
as I walk through
the pregnant air.

Insecurities . . .

The chimes in my yard
hang
in silent sorrow
until,
when the wind blows,
they sound
whispers in the day
and screams at night.

Black and White.

The photo-negative
of a dark-bearded white elf,
this old black man crouches forward
as he speaks.

His handshake
a dried out bag of bones
and arthritic knuckles,
he talks in circles
and he nods his head of white hair
in constant agreement.

He struggles to get his eyes
to focus or even to stay open.
Rather than expend the energy,
he remains half asleep in appearance.

The whites of his eyes never show
in his black, dry face.
The lines that accent his long, black hands
tell the difficult story of his past.

I wonder what he thinks
of the young, white man
who arrives weekly at his door
to play big brother to his neglected grandson.

Confessions of a Southern California Motorist.

Please forgive me for not stopping
when your car spun out and over the rail
down the embankment, rolling
then bouncing and landing upright.

I was 70 mph past you
racing toward a delivery deadline.

Your dust settled in my rear view mirror.

And forgive me for driving slowly
over your motorcycle's bent chrome gas tank,
slowly past your belly-down body
the torn flap of your jeans
covering your white thigh,
but not your white butt.

I meant to stop, to run over,
to check your pulse . . .

But the growing crowd circled
the perimeter of the scattered pieces
of your motorcycle,

and you bled into the asphalt,

and I drove sickened into the busy
nothingness of my life.

Getting Carried Away.

As a boy, I engineered a loud locomotive.
Nudged and shoved, my engine struggled
up an angry mountain.

Hot. Frustrated. Working.
When the mountain topped off,
my locomotive burned down the other side,
never running far enough to become exhausted,
never running out of words.

The boy I was shot hell-fire from his mouth
when he was confused.
Angry and unable to communicate
with adults who would not listen,
I yelled selfish listen-to-me-damnits
when the world turned its back.

I shook of energy
and learned to hate myself,
learned to hate the lack of translation,
and I was aggravated with adults who could not understand
the anxious burning inside me.

As an angry boy,
I screamed my secrets against the wall of the world.
I would catch the echo,
sling it over my shoulder
and carry myself away.

Coach Louie

Written by Lucas James McMaster

I was ten years old and it was the third day of my first year of Pop Warner football, and I was scared. I was sitting in my room, dreading practice. I didn't want to be yelled at again like I was at every other practice that I've been to. I didn't want Coach Louie to call me a girl and shove me to the ground and humiliate me. I started to get dressed, but I couldn't do it. I started to feel sick. I thought to myself *I'm just nervous.* But I wasn't nervous. I was scared shitless. I knew what would happen at practice and I knew there was nothing I could do about it. My head ached, my throat felt like sandpaper, and my stomach was doing cartwheels. A light went on in my head. I can't go to practice if I'm sick. I can't go to practice if I'm sick. *I can't go to practice.*

I got up and told my Mom I was sick. She took my temperature, ninety-nine degrees. She said it was my choice whether or not I went to practice. When she said that, I could tell that she knew what I was doing. I felt ashamed; I knew that I could go and that I could deal with Coach Louie. I was just being weak. I made myself sick because I was weak. I tried to get out of practice because I was weak. I would not be weak. I would go to practice.

I was small for my age and I knew it. Being on the football field didn't help me forget the size difference between me and the other boys.

And I hated it. It gave me an inferiority complex that I felt I couldn't do anything about. It also made me insanely competitive. I played football because my Dad had. He always said there was no pressure on me to play and however I did would be fine. But he had been a god at the game. What did he know about the failure I was sure to find on the football field? I had something to prove to myself as well as everyone else. Football was an entirely new world to me. I was unaccustomed to the yelling and vicious contact. But I stepped into that world ready to learn and to prove myself at all costs.

The tires scraped against the gravel of the back entrance to the practice field as we pulled up in our white, falling-apart Astro Van. I was late. Coach Louie and the rest of the team were already lined up and stretching. Coach Louie's booming voice could be heard even from the car. I sighed and got out of the car. I knew that Coach Louie wouldn't let me off easy for being late. He never let me off easy for anything. My Mom offered to walk me up to practice and say that it was her fault I was late. No, I couldn't do that. That would only make me look weaker to Coach Louie. Plus, I was ten. I was independent.

As soon as I set foot on the grass I knew Coach Louie had seen me. His voice boomed across the field, just as loud as if he was right next to me. "Well, would you look at that everyone. Looks as if Little Mac finally decided to show up." I didn't say anything; it wouldn't make a difference. I just ran across the grass to discover what new punishment Coach Louie would give me.

Coach Louie was this really big Mexican, six feet tall and had to weigh a good two hundred and fifty pounds. He had a beer belly he could rest his hands on and tattoos covered the length of his arms. He was a giant to me. He was always either laughing or yelling. He scared me.

I run up and Coach Louie yells at me to go ahead and keep on running. I finished up a lap of the entire field and got back to the team. Coach Louie yells again, Keep running. My breath isn't coming easy anymore but I keep going. The lap turns into three then four and Coach Louie won't let me stop. The rest of the team finished their stretches and I'm panting but I don't stop the killer pace I had set for myself. I couldn't let Coach Louie know that he was getting to me.

After five laps, Coach Louie let me stop. I'm sweating underneath the oppressive burden of my shoulder pads. My helmet never seemed so small. I go to the back of the line for the hitting drills that the team is doing. Coach

Louie sees me go to the back and starts laughing. "Get your ass up here, Little Mac. You ain't hiding back there."

I still haven't caught my breath but I go to the front to get it over with. It was the drill where two guys lay down on the grass head to head. One has the ball, then, on the whistle, they both get up and the guy with the ball tries to get past the guy who doesn't have the ball. It sounds simple but it was new to me. I looked to see who I was up against. Chad Musser. The Moose. He was the biggest guy on the team. He was not afraid of contact and he had played before. He was a good guy but I knew he wouldn't go easy on me. I looked at Coach Louie; he had a huge grin on his face. Coach Louie knew I had never played before and that this week was the first time I had been introduced to full contact. But I wasn't about to show my fear to him, so I got down for the drill. The whistle blew. I wasn't ready. I was barely up when Chad ran me over, hard. I got up to the sounds of laughter from my teammates. I was pissed at myself. With my head down and fists clenched I walked to the back of the line. "Where are you going, Little Mac? I'm not done with you yet," boomed Coach Louie. Of course he's not, I thought to myself.

I went back and it was the same thing, Chad running me over and me getting up slower than before. Again, says Coach Louie. I look at him and he is smiling. Ok, so I'll prove him wrong. Now, I'm really mad. I get up as fast as I can and again Chad is lower than me, and he trucks me. The team is no longer laughing. It's dead quiet. As I'm getting back up, I am shoved down from behind. I hit the ground hard. The grass no longer feels soft and pieces of it are stuck to my helmet. I get up to Coach Louie saying, "You might as well stay down there if your gonna keep going down that easy, Little Mac."

We finished that drill and started a new one called The Circle. Coach Louie had the entire team make a huge circle. Coach Louie said that he would put someone in the middle then walk around and have other people hit the guy in the middle at random. Coach Louie said that this would teach us not to be afraid of contact. He says this looking at me pointedly. Coach Louie puts me in The Circle first. I'm not surprised, but I am scared. I'm ashamed at myself for being scared. We start the drill, and I'm in the middle, pumping my feet trying to see where the first hit will come from. It comes from the side and I hit the ground. I pop back up only to be floored by a facemask. This cycle keeps going until after one particularly hard hit I'm slow to get up. Coach Louie is screaming, "What the hell is wrong with you? Are you a pussy? Are you a bitch? You are, aren't you?" Coach Louie is yelling at me but the words were in my head first. Coach Louie walks up to me, grabs my shoulder pads and hurls me to the ground. "You don't fall to the ground! You don't let me throw you to the ground!" He is right in my face, screaming. Flecks of spit fly from his mouth to my face. Coach Louie repeats the process of throwing me down. I feel so powerless to this giant. I feel so weak. Anger is welling in my chest, frustration pushing against my ribs. My head is ringing with his words. Maybe I am just weak. Maybe I'm just not good enough. Maybe I am too small.

NO. I refuse to be weak. I will not be weak. The anger at the injustice of Coach Louie's picking on me finally reached boiling point.

I get back up and as Coach Louie grabs at my shoulder pads again I pop his hands off and I tackle him with all my anger heading my attack. I hit him but I can't move him. He shoves me back, harder than before. I stumble back but don't fall. I renew my attack but Coach Louie just holds me back at arms length. I stop fighting and look up to see Coach Louie grinning. "That's what I want to see Big Mac," says Coach Louie. Big Mac. That was me. That was the first compliment Coach Louie had ever given me. And it meant more to me than any other compliment I have ever received.

The rest of the practice was as if an entirely new world had been opened up to me. I was no longer scared to get hit or to hit and it showed. I played with a newfound ferocity. A fire had been lit inside of me and that was something no one could take from me. During the rest of the hitting drills I turned heads. To my teammates I was no longer the scared little kid that hung to the back of the group. I was Big Mac, the insane white boy who tackled with reckless disregard for his own physical well-being. At the end of practice when Coach Louie tortured us with a half an hour of straight running and one hundred leg raises, I ran with the head of the pack and outlasted everyone else.

After practice I almost didn't want to take off my pads. They had become like an extension of my body. My helmet was no longer uncomfortable. It seemed right, like it belonged on my head. I felt naked without my pads. But the fire inside me didn't leave when I took off my pads and walked off the field.

As I was walking I realized the change inside of me. I knew that I would no longer watch life happen to me. I had power. I had willpower and the power of my anger. I was no longer afraid, not of Coach Louie, not of being picked on, not of life. I was no longer concerned about my size. Size didn't matter as much as heart and I knew that I was not lacking in that area. I was in control of myself and that was enough.

CPSIA information can be obtained
at www.ICGtesting.com
Printed in the USA
FSOW02n1259210315
5893FS